Rings, Kings, and Butterflies

Rings, Kings, and Butterflies

Lessons on Christian Symbols for Children
with CD-ROM

Harriet VanderMeer
Illustrated by Elizabeth Steele Halstead

Augsburg Fortress
MINNEAPOLIS

To all the children—great and grand

RINGS, KINGS, AND BUTTERFLIES
Lessons on Christian Symbols for Children
with accompanying CD

Large-quantity purchases or custom editions of this book are available at a discount from the publisher. For more information, contact the sales department at Augsburg Fortress, Publishers, 1-800-328-4648, or write to: Sales Director, Augsburg Fortress, Box 1209, Minneapolis, MN 55440.

Scripture passages are from the *New Revised Standard Version* of the Bible, copyright © 1946, 1952, 1971, 1989 by the Division of Christian Education of the National Council of the Churches of Christ in the U.S.A. Used by permission.

Library of Congress Cataloging-in-Publication Data
VanderMeer, Harriet, 1944-
  Rings, kings & butterflies! : lessons on Christian symbols for children / by Harriet VanderMeer ; illustrated by Elizabeth Steele Halstead.
     p. cm.
  Includes bibliographical references and index.
  ISBN 0-8066-4931-3 (pbk. with cdrom : alk. paper)
  1. Christian art and symbolism—Study and teaching (Elementary) 2. Church year—Study and teaching (Elementary) 3. Worship (Religious education) I. Title: Rings, kings, and butterflies!. II. Halstead, Elizabeth Steele. III. Title.

  BV150.V36 2006
  268'.432—dc22   2006004766

Cover design by Diana Running; Book design by Michelle L. N. Cook

The paper used in this publication meets the minimum requirements of American National Standard for Information Sciences—Permanence of Paper for Printed Library Materials, ANSI Z329.48-1984. ⊚ ™

Manufactured in the U.S.A.

10   09   08   07   06   1   2   3   4   5   6   7   8   9   10

Contents

Introduction

Applicability of Curriculum

This collection of messages is designed for individuals or groups involved with teaching principles of the Christian faith to children. It is intended for church pastors, youth ministers, church school, parochial and home school teachers. Other groups and individuals, such as parents, grandparents, or other caregivers can use the lessons as they teach children about religion.

Time Frame for Use of Curriculum

This book of children's messages and activities contains 56 lessons—a lesson for each Sunday of the year plus special holidays. The lessons begin with Advent and follow the liturgical year. The symbols for each season are listed alphabetically and can be used anytime during the season.

Church Calendar

The liturgical year has six seasons: Advent, Christmas, Epiphany, Lent, Easter, and Pentecost. Some seasons are fixed, like Christmas, which always begins on December 25 and lasts for twelve days, placing Epiphany on January 6 every year. Other seasons, such as Easter, are set by factors dependent upon natural phenomena, such as the date of the spring equinox or full moon, which changes the dates of some holidays from one year to the next.

Lesson Overview

These lessons are organized around the seasons of the liturgical year. Each season includes an introduction and background information. Each of the 56 lessons features one Christian symbol/motif, which is illustrated and defined by the season color, themes, background information, Old and New Testament references, and applications for children. Each lesson includes an object to use, goals for the lesson, Bible texts to learn, a message, a prayer, appropriate musical selections, and a follow-up activity for children. Each lesson can be applied in a church, school, or home setting, lasting five minutes, an hour, or can be expanded to a week.

Symbols/Motifs

The symbols/motifs used in the lessons represent Christian symbols rooted in the Old and New Testaments and reflect Christian theological or historical traditions. Themes such as the providence, majesty, and universality of God, the creation, sacrifice, and atonement of Christ, and the illumination of the Holy Spirit are used. Objects from the world of nature, objects from the past and present, and objects surrounding us are used to give meaning to the symbols/motifs. By following the lessons sequentially throughout the year, children will learn a broad spectrum of Christian symbols and motifs.

Visual Aids/Woodcuts

For each lesson, visual aids are suggested to help children understand the meaning of the symbol/motif. Some of the objects could be found in the church sanctuary, or objects may be brought in to the lesson. The messages in this collection are accompanied with a woodcut depicting each symbol.

Recommendations

Keep the lesson simple; the attention spans of children are limited. In a church service, the lesson should be short, no more than five minutes. Use only one idea with one object in a lesson. Keep the message clear; visual aids are extremely helpful for children to see, touch, or smell. Use an intriguing statement to grab the children's interest when introducing the lesson. Use direct questions seldom; time and attention is lost while waiting for everyone to answer. Tell a story or read a story; children love to hear stories.

The message should be appropriate to the church season and the general theme of the service. It should be meaningful to the entire congregation. The leader should use a microphone or speak loudly enough so the message can be heard by everyone. The leader should choose an appropriate seating arrangement for the children when they come to hear the message; decide beforehand if the children or the leader should face the congregation.

Using the CD-ROM

The CD-ROM that accompanies this book includes the following features:

- Downloadable images of the seasonal art pieces provided in two sizes: one size for display and demonstration purposes, and another smaller size for use in creating mailings, newsletters, and take-home sheets.
- Downloadable appendices that will assist you in planning related to the church year calendar. Summaries of church year colors and symbols, as well as various ways the symbols relate to Bible references are included.

Use your imagination with the resources listed on the CD-ROM. For example, use the lists to create your own "Seasons and Symbols Matching Game." List symbols and have students try to match them to the appropriate season.

Acknowledgments

Family and friends for their support.

My parents for their interest in music, ideas, and religion.

My kids for their love and hope in the past and future.

Betsy for her art work and ideas; Reinder for his expertise.

And Jim for being there.

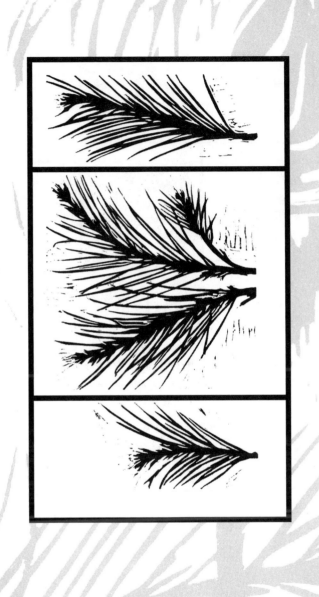

Season
of Advent

Season of Advent

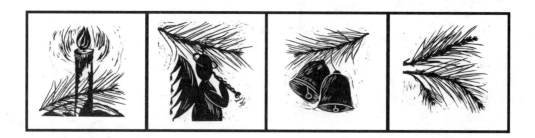

About the Time

The four Sundays before Christmas Eve, beginning the Sunday nearest St. Andrew's Day, November 30, and ending Christmas Eve

Seasonal Color

Purple or blue

Advent Themes

Beginning of the church year, call to worship
Personal preparation for Jesus' birth
Joyful anticipation of Christ's second coming
Celebration of the hope, peace, love, and joy Jesus brings to the world
Christ's incarnation brings light and life to the world.

About the Season

With Advent, the church year begins. Advent Sunday, the first Sunday of Advent, is the Sunday closest to St. Andrews Day, November 30. Secular calendars change every year, so the date of Advent Sunday falls between November 27 and December 3. The season of Advent itself varies in length from 22 to 28 days, ending Christmas Eve.

Observance of Advent originated in France during the fourth century as a time of preparation for church membership prior to baptism on Epiphany. During the fifth century, the length of the season varied from three to seven weeks of preparation for membership or for Christmas. By the sixth century, the Romans set the season to have four Sundays, and in the eleventh century, Gregory VII decreed that the standard of Advent for the whole church would be four Sundays. During the Middle Ages, penitence was added to the emphasis on preparation. Today the season is looked upon as a time of personal reflection and introspection—preparation through penitence, prayer, and patience.

The word *advent* originated from two Latin words: *ad* (to or toward) and *venire* (to come), thus "to come toward." The word connotes the joyful anticipation of Christ coming to our world. We celebrate three aspects of the "coming":

1. The coming of Christ in human form,
2. the coming of Christ in Word and Spirit, and
3. the second coming of Christ in glory at the end of the world.

Advent directs the church to examine the historical events surrounding Jesus' birth, to reflect on the revelation of Christ in Scripture, and to look ahead to Christ's final return. We prepare and hope for the entrance of Christ into this world and the next. The liturgical color of Advent is purple, which symbolizes the dignity and royalty but also the sorrow and penitence of Christ. The color blue, symbolizing hope, may also be used during Advent.

The Advent wreath symbolizes watchfulness and anticipation as the Lord's nativity approaches. The wreath has four outer candles, now usually purple or blue, but traditionally white. These candles have been given names. The Prophecy candle announces the period of waiting; the Bethlehem candle symbolizes the preparations being made to receive and cradle the Christ child;

the Shepherd's candle typifies the act of sharing Christ; the Angel's candle symbolizes love and Christ's final coming. Sometimes the candles are simply called the candles of hope, love, joy, and peace. A fifth candle sits in the center of the wreath and is lit on Christmas Eve or Day. This white Christ candle reminds us that Christ is the light of the world. Lighting one more of the four candles each week of Advent symbolizes the increasing amount of light spread to the world as Jesus' coming approaches. The wreath is without ornamentation, and its circle represents eternity. It is evergreen (fir, spruce, balsam, or pine), representing the eternal life through Christ, God's gift to us.

Key Bible Texts
Old Testament: Isaiah 9:2
New Testament: John 8:12; Matthew 5:14-16

Advent for Children
The lighting of the Advent wreath, a ring of evergreen branches with four purple or blue candles, is a familiar custom during this season. The first candle represents hope, the second represents peace, the third represents love, and the fourth represents joy. A white Christ candle sits in the center. One more of the colored candles is lit each Sunday until the last Sunday in Advent, when all of them are lit. The Christ candle is lit on Christmas Eve or Christmas Day to proclaim that Christ, the light of the world, is born.

Advent 1

Symbol/Motif: angel

Object: a clay, wood, ceramic, or lace angel

Throughout the Bible, from the Garden of Eden to the book of Revelation, angels appear as God's messengers. Angels proclaim events; they provide guidance, help, and counsel; they predict things to come; and they explain and carry out God's judgments. Angels also represent the image of God: watchful, loving, and protective. Some angels are given names, others suggest a connection to the deity, and some have fallen.

Goal

See the roles angels play in the Christmas story and other Bible stories.

Bible Texts

Old Testament: Daniel 6:22, Psalm 91:11, Isaiah 6:3
New Testament: Matthew 1:20, Luke 2:9-14, Revelation 8

Verse to Learn

And suddenly there was with the angel a multitude of the heavenly host, praising God and saying, "Glory to God in the highest heaven, and on earth peace among those whom he favors." Luke 2:13-14

A Children's Message

You can put many things on top of your Christmas tree. Some people put a star there and some put a big bow. Some people put a bird up there or their favorite decoration. One of the most beautiful decorations for the top of the tree is an angel. With an angel on top of your tree, you proclaim with the angel that Jesus is coming!

Angels are messengers. Sometimes angels sing their message, sometimes they shout, sometimes they play instruments, sometimes they whisper, and sometimes they are quiet. Angels appear to tell a story or make an announcement. They say, "Fear not!" or they shout, "Behold!" or they sing, "Holy, Holy, Holy." There are angels of proclamation with a forceful message. There are angels of protection, who quietly surround you, guard you, and take care of you. People sometimes refer to "an angel on my shoulder watching over me." Angels guided the Israelites out of the wilderness. They were guardian angels.

There are also praising angels in the Bible, who show us how to worship and praise God. We sing as they did when we sing, "Holy, Holy, Holy, Lord God Almighty." Little angels are sometimes called "cherubs." A young children's choir may be called a "cherub choir," because they look and act like cherubs.

The Advent and Christmas stories are filled with angels. A proclamation angel comes to announce the forerunner of Jesus, John the Baptist. A pronouncing angel tells Mary that she will have a baby, Jesus. Praising angels give the message to the shepherds to go to Bethlehem to see the newborn king. Singing angels sing, "Glory to God in the Highest." A messenger angel tells Joseph to leave and take the baby to Egypt. And finally, when Herod dies and it is safe, a guardian angel takes Jesus back to Israel.

During this Advent season, we need to look for all the angels around us: angels of preparation, telling us to get ready for Jesus; angels of promise, telling us Jesus is coming; angels of praise, showing us how to worship Jesus; angels of patience, teaching us how to search and wait for him; angels of proclamation, announcing the birth of Jesus. Christmas trees are exciting to get and fun to decorate. Instead of looking to see what is under the tree, put an angel on top of your tree. Then raise your head, look, and listen. Do you hear the angel whispering, "Gloria in Excelsis Deo"?

Pray with Children

Dear God, may we hear your angels as they proclaim Jesus' birth. May we join the angels in praising you this Christmas season, and sing with them throughout the year. Amen

Related Music

"Angels We Have Heard on High," Edward S. Barnes
"Hark! The Herald Angels Sing," Charles Wesley
"Angels from the Realms of Glory," James Montgomery

To Do Together

Look through your books, Christmas cards, and in some stores to see how angels are depicted. Do they have wings and halos? What color are their robes? Where they are located in the picture? Draw or make a variety of angels to decorate your Christmas tree or wrapping paper. Make and display a collage of the angels from past years' Christmas cards.

Advent 2

Symbol/Motif: bells

Object: Christmas bells, handbells, sleigh bells, or other bells

Bells ring as a call to worship God and as a proclamation of the gospel to the world. In the Old Testament, bells were part of the worship of God and served as adornments on the robes of priests.

Goal

Enjoy bells as symbols of the call to worship and the proclamation of the good news to the world.

Bible Texts

Old Testament: Exodus 39:25-26
New Testament: Acts 9:15

Verse to Learn

Praise the LORD! Praise God in his sanctuary. . . . Let everything that breathes praise the LORD. Praise the LORD! Psalm 150:1, 6

A Children's Message

Everywhere you go you hear bells. Listen for them. Each bell tells you something different. A fire engine rings its bell on the way to a fire. A school bell rings when its time for school to begin. A farmer might put a bell on a cow so that, when the cow roams, it won't get lost. Sleigh bells ring when you go for a sleigh ride. Salvation Army bells ring to announce that others need your help at Christmas. Church bells ring when it's time to go to church.

Each time these bells ring, they tell you that something is happening. It makes you stop and listen . . . and maybe hurry. It used to be that when the town bells rang, it was a signal that something had happened, and that people should come gather to find out. The bell on your stove rings to signal that the cookies are done. Hurry or they will burn. Your alarm clock bell rings and it says "get up." A bell often gives you a signal that something is happening: Stop. Wake up. You'd better get going!

Imagine a little cabin out in the woods, out in the middle of nowhere. There is not another house nearby, or any other people in sight. It is very quiet and peaceful. Down the road a ways is a tiny, old chapel—with bells that ring. At quarter after the hour, just four bells ring; at half past the hour, eight bells ring; at quarter to the hour, twelve bells ring; and at the hour, all twelve bells ring, plus a bell rings for each hour of the day to tell you what hour it is. At 6:00 in the evening, special bells, called the *Angelicas,* ring. Many times a day the bells ring, calling people to church or just to stop what they're doing and say a prayer. Imagine walking in the woods and hearing those bells ring. Would you stop, and maybe say a little prayer?

Hanging little bells on a Christmas tree reminds us that this season is really about Jesus, and bells announce his birth. It doesn't matter whether it is brass bells or lace bells or sleigh bells or church bells. They all announce good cheer, joy, and love because Jesus is born. And in this season, we sing carols about bells as well as ring them. A favorite carol is "I Heard the Bells on Christmas Day." For us bells tell us to, "Stop. Look. Listen." And then say, "Go tell it on the mountain that Jesus Christ is born!"

Pray with Children
Dear God, may bells call us to worship you. May bells ring in the good news of your Son's birth. May bells sing with joy and praise to your glory and honor. Amen

Related Music
"I Heard the Bells on Christmas Day," J. Baptiste Calkin
"On Christmas Night," Traditional English
"Go Tell It on the Mountain," African American spiritual

To Do Together
Learn the J. Calkin carol with words written by Henry W. Longfellow, "I Heard the Bells on Christmas Day." Sing the song as a prayer at mealtime or bedtime. Pray for peace on earth, good will to all.

Advent 3

Symbol/Motif: candle

Object: a candle

In Bible times, light often referred to the divine presence and holiness of God. In the New Testament, light symbolizes the light and life Christ brought into the world. That light's radiance and glow signify his holy presence in the world. Jesus is identified as the light of the world who gives eternal life to God's people. Believers are called "children of light" and are the bearers of divine light.

Goal
Identify Jesus as the light of the world.

Bible Texts
Old Testament: Genesis 1:3-4, Psalm 27:1, Isaiah 9:2
New Testament: Matthew 5:16, John 1:4-5, Revelation 22:5

Verse to Learn
Let your light shine before others, so that they may see your good works and give glory to your Father in heaven. Matthew 5:16

A Children's Message
Do you ever need someone to help you? Have you ever asked someone to "shed some light" on a problem to solve it? When you are "in the dark" about a problem, you can't figure it out on our

own. A problem can be too big even for parents to solve. Problems can seem so big that no one in the whole world could solve them. Sometimes we need help to crawl out of darkness and step into the light.

Have you ever been in total darkness, when it's so dark you can almost touch it or feel it? It can be scary. At the creation of the world, God said, "Let there be light" (Genesis 1:3). And the light was good, just as God said! It's so good that we wouldn't be here without light. We cannot live without light, because nothing grows without light. God gives us the light and warmth of the sun so that everything can live and grow. But God is our main source of light, shedding light on us, everyone around us, every animal, plant, and flower, and every star in the sky. Throughout our lives and beyond, we have someone who sheds light on our world, someone who solves our problems and someone who saves us! No problem is too big for the God who created light.

When Jesus was on the earth, he said, "I am the light of the world" (John 8:12). Later he said, "And there will be no more night; they need no light of lamp or sun, for the Lord God will be their light!" (Revelation 22:5). While Jesus was on earth, he told us to be lights of the world. He said, "You are the light of the world. Let your light shine before others, so that they may see your good works and give glory to your Father in heaven" (Matthew 5:14,16). What an assignment!

The Advent wreath helps us prepare for Jesus and for being lights in the world. We can be lights because Jesus shares his light with us. He gives us light for every season of the year, for every day of the year. As we light each Advent candle, may we see his light, be a light, and share our light with everyone around us. We will then be the children of light who can say, "The Lord is my light and my salvation; whom shall I fear?" (Psalm 27:1). No one and nothing.

Pray with Children

Dear God, you are the light of our world. Without you we live in darkness. Give us the vision to see your light. Teach us to follow that light. We thank you for shedding your light in our world. Amen

Related Music

"This Little Light of Mine," African American spiritual
"The Lord Is My Light and My Salvation," Frances Allitsen
"Break Forth, O Beauteous Heavenly Light," J. S. Bach

To Do Together

Decorate your family table with an Advent wreath. Light a candle each night during dinner and sing a Christmas carol. Before bedtime, light a candle while you say the Verse to Learn, Matthew 5:16. Sing, "This Little Light of Mine." Give thanks to Jesus for lighting our world.

Advent 4

Symbol/Motif: evergreens

Object: an evergreen branch

The color green appears at creation when God gives the animals green plants to eat. It also appears after the flood when God gives Noah green plants for food. Ever since then, green has been associated with life, fruitfulness, and abundance. Green represents the beauty and color of vegetative life and the best of the natural world. The evergreen tree always stays green and is associated with God's favor and love.

Goal

Recognize the evergreen as a symbol of life throughout the year.

Bible Texts

Old Testament: Genesis 1:30, Psalm 23:2, Genesis 2
New Testament: Revelation 22:2, Mark 6:39, and Revelation 8:7

Verse to Learn

Blessed are those who trust in the LORD, whose trust is the LORD. They shall be like a tree planted by water, sending out its roots by the stream. Jeremiah 17:7-8

A Children's Message

Getting a Christmas tree is exciting. There are so many things to think about: Where do we find a tree? A tree farm, a field, maybe a grocery store, or a gas station? What kind will it be? A balsam fir, a spruce, a white pine? Which one has the best shape? Which one keeps its needles the longest? Then you need to find the decorations and turn on the stereo with Christmas music—so loud that it can be heard in every room inside and even outside—while you decorate. Once the decorations are in place, the wreath is on the door, Christmas music is on the piano, stockings are on the mantel, nativity sets are on the shelves, and packages are under the tree; the official Christmas season has begun! Christmas is no longer coming; it's here!

Why is that evergreen tree so important? Every Christmas tree you see this season—big or little, dense or sparse, balsam or pine—each one came from God. God nurtures every tree—maples and oaks, fruit trees and flowering trees, pines and palm trees. God makes the reds and yellows of autumn trees, the whites of blossoming spring trees, and all the green trees of summer. Trees give us fruit and shade and beauty. All are from God.

Your Christmas tree started as a seedling. It was watered and nurtured along the way. The green, bushy Christmas tree prepares the way for the birth of Jesus in Bethlehem. But the Christmas tree also promises us the tree of Good Friday: the bare tree that became a cross for

Jesus to die on. Jesus came into the world and saved us from the world, and our Christmas trees remind us of that promise.

Jesus comes to us at Christmas, but he saves us at Easter. That is why Advent is so exciting: We are getting ready for Christmas, and we are getting ready for Easter. The Christmas tree shows you the Christ who gives us everlasting life, because under it, wrapped in swaddling clothes, is the gift of Jesus. We need to prepare our gifts and ourselves for him.

Pray with Children
Dear God, as we prepare for Christmas, may our Christmas tree be at the center of our homes and remind us that you are the tree of life. We thank you for Jesus, and in his name. Amen

Related Music
"O Christmas Tree," Traditional German
"When We Walk With the Lord," Daniel B. Towner
"Lo, How a Rose E'er Blooming," Michael Praetorius

To Do Together
Look for as many different kinds of evergreen trees as you can, in your neighborhood, park, or local arboretum. While shopping for a Christmas tree and a Christmas wreath, notice what kind of evergreen needles and pinecones they have. Talk about God's nature and love embodied in that tree.

Season
of Christmas

Season of Christmas

About the Time

Christmas Day and the following 12 days, including the Sunday after Christmas (Christmas Sunday); December 25 through January 5

Seasonal Color

White

Christmas Themes

Jesus' birth into the Holy Family
God Incarnate, light of the world, the Messiah
God's ultimate gift—the Son and Savior

About the Season

The Christmas season begins on Christmas Day, December 25, and lasts for 12 days, through January 5, the eve of Epiphany, sometimes called "Twelfth Night." The liturgical color for the season of Christmas is white, symbolizing purity, radiant light, supernatural brilliance, and transcendent reality. The season is also called the Celebration of the Incarnation or the Nativity of Our Lord.

In the history of the church, Christmas observance began centuries after Jesus was born. In fact, many of the popular symbols of the Christmas season, such as the evergreen tree, the Yule log, holly, pine, bay, laurel, and ivy, originated in the pagan world. Earlier traditions combined the season of harvest with the preparation of food, shelter, and heat for the coming winter months, which were essential for survival. The high point of the celebration was the winter solstice, when pagan gods were called upon to help the people.

In the early church, the birth date of Jesus was hardly observed, whereas his resurrection was considered very important. As significant as his birth for the early church was his baptism by John the Baptist. Celebrated on January 6, the twelfth day after Christmas, Epiphany also honors the Wise Men who arrived in Bethlehem to present their gifts. During the fourth century, however, the newly Christianized Romans appropriated the winter solstice, December's shortest day of the year, which signified the rebirth of the sun, as the day to celebrate the birth of Jesus. Telesphorus, the second bishop of Rome (A.D. 129-138), determined that the holy night of the Nativity should be celebrated in public church services or masses, and Theophilus, Bishop of Caesarea, declared that that celebration should occur on the 25th of December. This decree created some controversy, and not until A.D. 325-350 was December 25 officially designated as Christmas and a church festival.

In the sixth century, Dionysius Exiguus, a Roman monk, conducted an investigation to determine the exact year in which Jesus was born. It was his idea to divide history into two eras, B.C. and A.D., with the birth date of Jesus the dividing point. He determined that Jesus was born in the year 754 of the Roman calendar. Our calendar is based on this conclusion. However, evidence in New Testament and archaeological findings do not corroborate this conclusion. The year 7 B.C., or the Roman year 747, appears to be the actual year of Jesus' birth.

Early Christianity grew alongside many pagan cultures, and sometimes adapted pagan understandings and practices. For example, pagan worship of the sun became Christian worship of the Son of Righteousness. Eventually, Christians developed more interest in the circumstances surrounding the birth of Jesus, a flesh-and-blood figure. Jesus' birth became a focus of faith, as did his mother, Mary, a saint who received homage as the blessed Virgin.

Key Bible Texts

Old Testament: 2 Samuel 7:8, Isaiah 9:6, Micah 5:2
New Testament: Matthew 1:18–2:14; Luke 2; John 1:1-18

Christmas for Children

The word *Christmas* is a combination of the two words *Christ* and *mass*, the name given to the worship service on December 25. Christmas is a season of great joy, with singing of Christmas carols, reading of the story of Jesus' birth, and giving of gifts to symbolize the greatest gift, God's Son.

Christmas 1

Symbol/Motif: natal star

Object: many different stars, including a four-point star and a cross of the same size

The natal star (with four points) represents the birth of Christ and symbolizes the light his birth and life brought into the world. The natal star also reflects the earthly mission Jesus took on when he entered the world as the Son of Man. The four points of the star remind us of the four points of the cross Jesus will bear on Good Friday. Both his birth and death are represented in this natal star, fulfilling biblical star-related prophecies.

Goal
Recognize the importance and significance of the four-pointed natal star.

Bible Texts
Old Testament: Numbers 24:17, Psalm 148:3, Job 38:7
New Testament: Matthew 2:2, 1 Corinthians 15:41, Revelation 1:16

Verse to Learn
When they had heard the king, they set out; and there, ahead of them, went the star that they had seen at its rising, until it stopped over the place where the child was. When they saw that the star had stopped, they were overwhelmed with joy. Matthew 2:9-10

A Children's Message

If you go out on a dark night you will see millions of stars—so many stars that you may agree with the animated character, Buzz Lightyear, who says, "to infinity and beyond." Astronomers talk about the Milky Way and Arcturus while non-astronomers sing about little twinkling stars, the evening star, and the morning star, and read about Hollywood stars, athletic stars, and galactic stars.

There are more stars in the sky than we can count; and we can't count the points on those stars either. But when we draw stars, we give them a specific number of points—three, four, five, seven, or maybe twelve. Our stars are earthly stars, made with paper, lace, or clay to represent something heavenly.

Like astronomers who name heavenly stars such as the North Star, we give names to kinds of stars. We have named a star with four points the "natal star." The word *natal* in Latin means birth. The "neo-natal" nursery in the hospital is for the tiniest newborn babies. The four-point star is called the Christ star or the natal star because it is associated with Jesus' birth. When you see this natal star, think of Jesus, the manger, and the whole nativity scene because *nativity* comes from *natal* too. Jesus is like a star from heaven falling to earth to light our world from that lowly manger. Instead of "to infinity and beyond!" he is *from* infinity to us.

This natal star represents both the birth of Jesus and his mission here on earth: He was sent by God to save us from our sins. Where does Jesus die? On a cross. Extend each of these four points out straight and what shape do you have? A cross. Jesus was born a human being like us, but also to be our savior. That is why the natal star has the same shape as the cross. The natal star shows us God's promise that Jesus is born, and also shows us that Jesus will die—for us. That natal star shines brightly in heaven, signaling that Jesus came for us and his light lights the world. We need to be like the Wise Men and follow that star wherever it takes us. Look for it. Wait for it. Believe it. Love it.

Pray with Children

Dear God, shine for us and show us the way. May our hearts and lives shine with your light. Make us grateful for the birth and love of Jesus. Amen

Related Music

"Star of the East," Amanda Kennedy
"O Come, Little Children," J. A. Schulz
"Rise Up, Shepherd, and Follow," African American spiritual

To Do Together

Cut paper of many different colors into squares. Fold two of the corners of each back to look like a paper airplane. Arrange groups of eight of them in the shape of a star and glue or tape them together. Punch a hole in one of the points, loop ribbon or string through, and tie. Hang the star on your Christmas tree or in a window.

Christmas 2

Symbol/Motif: the nativity

Object: a crèche

The nativity scene includes the star above symbolizing the divine; and the manger, shepherds, animals, holy family, and Wise Men in the stable symbolizing the earthly aspects of the story.

Goal

Become familiar with the Christmas story, of God Incarnate coming to earth.

Bible Texts

Old Testament: Isaiah 9:6
New Testament: Matthew 1:23

Verse to Learn

And she gave birth to her firstborn son and wrapped him in bands of cloth, and laid him in a manger, because there was no place for them in the inn. Luke 2:7

A Children's Message

As we prepare for Christmas, we sing, "It's the most wonderful time of the year . . ." It is also the most wonderful feeling of the year, the most wonderful story of the year. And Christmas is the most wonderful day of the year!

This box, called a crèche, shows us why this is the most wonderful day of the year. The story is completely earthly, and completely heavenly. Even though the crèche is a little box, it holds a huge, magnificent story. Even though the story is about ordinary people and ordinary things, it is really the most extraordinary event in history. And even though the event didn't get front-page news coverage, it marked the most important date in history. We can tell it happened at night because there are stars in heaven. One special star, bigger and brighter than all the others, gives light to everyone inside and everyone outside. There are angels and that tells us this is not an everyday occurrence; it is something special. Listen. The angels singing heavenly music, "Glory to God!" can be heard for miles around, all over the earth.

For such an important event, this box should be a palace! But it's not; it is a very plain stable. For such an important event, there should be reporters covering the story. But they are nowhere to be found. For such an important event, there should be lots of people. But there's only a mom, a dad, and a couple of shepherds. For such an important baby, there should be doctors and nurses. But there weren't any of those either. There are just some cows and sheep. For such an important birth, there should be blankets and clothes and maybe a space heater. But there is nothing for him.

Imagine being there. Listen. Can you hear Mary singing with the angels? They're all singing the *Magnificat*, a word which means "to magnify and glorify." Now that might be the most wonderful word of the year! It means that little baby Jesus is the most magnificent, most important person in this world. He is larger than all of us put together. In fact, he's larger than life. Jesus is Mary's son, but Jesus is also the Son of God and the Savior of the world. Look and listen. It's the holiest day of the year, and it's a scene that lasts all year long!

Pray with Children
Dear Jesus, thank you for your nativity and for coming to us on this most wonderful day of the year. Help us be a part of the Christmas scene each day of the year, praising and thanking you. Amen

Related Music
"Angels We Have Heard on High," French carol
"In the Bleak Midwinter," Gustav T. Holst
"Away in a Manger," William J. Kirkpatrick

To Do Together
Set out a nativity set that children can look at and play with. Read the story of Jesus' birth from the Bible, children's Bibles, and storybooks. Imagine being various members of the nativity scene. Act out the story with everyone playing different roles.

Season of Epiphany

Season of Epiphany

About the Time
Seven or eight Sundays, starting January 6 and ending 64 days before Easter

Seasonal Color
White or green

Epiphany Themes
Jesus, the manifestation of God and light in the world
Jesus, the precious jewel, the morning star
God's love for children of all ages
God, the creator of the world
The Holy Spirit's peace and love for us

About the Season

Epiphany is a Greek word meaning "manifestation," a showing forth, a disclosure, a revelation, an insight. For Christians, *epiphany* means God's "showing forth" to the world through Jesus. God brings Jesus to earth at Christmas, and during the season of Epiphany we see Jesus' works.

The Epiphany season commemorates the fulfillment of Christ to the Gentiles. The Wise Men, who followed the star to the child Jesus and presented their gifts, represent all the non-Jews for whom Christ came to earth. This birthday celebration begins the Epiphany season on January 6th. Epiphany begins in January, with the new calendar year. The name *January* comes from the Roman deity Janus, who has two faces: one looking back on the past and one peering ahead into the future and unknown experiences. During Epiphany we look back and then forward to the final page of the Christmas story.

Epiphany suggests a journey or pilgrimage, the setting of a new course, a grand spiritual odyssey. *Epiphany* implies a movement from ignorance to insight, from darkness to revelation, from the unknown to realization. Stories of epiphany, manifestation, and recognition are found throughout the Bible. In the Old Testament, these stories include Abraham and Isaac on Mt. Moriah, Jacob receiving the covenant blessing at Bethel, Jacob wrestling with the angel, and the story of Job. In the New Testament, epiphany stories include the disciples recognizing Jesus as the Lord, as well as Jesus' miracles. The Bible contains many epiphanies of God as the creator and ruler of the world, and of Jesus as God's beloved Son and Savior of the world.

At Jesus' baptism, which is celebrated during Epiphany, the Holy Spirit descends like a dove to earth. In the Bible, the dove also represents God's peace, covenant with God, and sacrifice to God. The dove carries an olive branch, is presented as a gift, and wears a halo with three rays, symbolizing the Holy Spirit. Through the Holy Spirit, Christians experience safety, beauty, peace, and eternal life.

The season of Epiphany begins as the Wise Men present their gifts of gold, frankincense, and myrrh. These gifts symbolize the role Jesus plays in God's plan: his kingship, sacrifice, and death. Along with the shepherds, these kings show the spreading of Christ's gifts to all people. As we anticipate our Epiphany journey into the future, we need to prepare our gifts and present them.

Epiphany, therefore, becomes a season of mission: a time for each church and its members to formulate, examine, and execute a mission statement. During Epiphany we celebrate the gifts we receive, and are called to share them. While the color white symbolizes the purity of the Trinity, liturgical green represents the fertility, growth, and joy we experience through the sharing of our gifts.

Key Bible Texts
Old Testament: Genesis 8:6-12, Psalm 2:7, Isaiah 43:1
New Testament: Luke 3:21-22

Epiphany for Children
The season of Epiphany brings light to all people, and so reveals Jesus, God's Son, as the light of the world. Jesus and the Holy Spirit come to us and for us, inspiring us to use our gifts to spread the light and further God's mission in the world for all humanity.

Epiphany/ Transfiguration

Symbol/Motif: children

Object: a pencil box and a lunchbox

There are over five hundred references to children in the Bible. Often childhood represents innocence and simplicity while adulthood represents maturity and wisdom. However, in some texts, children serve as models of faith for adults. Although the Bible identifies children as blessings from God, meant to be loved and cherished, it also suggests that they are in need of learning, discipline, nurture, and protection. Jesus makes time to bless children who are brought to him.

Goal
Recognize that just as children need tools for school they also need tools to grow in Christian faith.

Bible Texts
Old Testament: Deuteronomy 6:4-9, Proverbs 20:11
New Testament: Luke 9:46-48, Matthew 18:3-5, Luke 10:21, Mark 10:14, 1 Corinthians 13:11

Verse to Learn
"Love the Lord your God with all your heart, and with all your soul, and with all your mind, and with all your strength" (Mark 12:30). "Recite this to your children and talk about [it] when you are at home and when you are away, when you lie down and when you rise" (Deuteronomy 6:7).

A Children's Message

A carpenter has a toolbox filled with tools when going to work; sometimes a carpenter has an entire truck filled with tools and equipment. A doctor has a toolkit of sorts too: it's a black medical bag filled with tools needed to examine a patient. Firefighters have an entire fire engine filled with tools. Just as these people have tools for their jobs, there are many tools we need to help us grow in faith.

This special box is filled with things you need on your way to becoming a good Christian. It holds letters and numbers for you to learn so you can read and count, shapes for doing puzzles, pencils for writing, and all kinds of books. It also contains food to help your body grow and become strong. And a heart in your toolbox will remind you that you are loved—by your family, by your friends, and by God. How will each of these things help your faith grow?

What else should we keep in a box of tools like this? How about a Bible, so we can read the story of God's love for us? And a cross for sure; we need to know that Jesus died for us and trust that his promise of salvation is true. A little shepherd's staff can remind us of Jesus' love and care for us. Keep a heart in your toolbox, too. Jesus said that wherever you are—in school, on the playground, at home, or on a walk—you are to love the Lord your God with your whole heart and mind and soul, and love your neighbors as yourself. This was his commandment: to love. When you share your heart with others, you share it with Jesus.

With a toolbox like this, filled with all of these tools, we know that we are God's children, growing in love and faith.

Pray with Children

Dear God, you gave us Jesus, who taught us what to love, when to love, whom to love, and how to love. Help us to follow his example as we are nurtured by your love. Amen

Related Music

"Jesus Loves Me," William Bradbury
"Jesus Loves Even Me," Philip Bliss

To Do Together

Gather items for a personal faith toolbox. Include many sources of information and inspiration, including words, music, and art. Add to the box throughout your lives.

Epiphany 2

Symbol/Motif: dove

Object: a wood, clay, or cloth dove, or a picture of a dove

The Holy Spirit was present at the baptism of Jesus in the form of a dove, and since then the dove has been a symbol for the Holy Spirit. God used the dove as a symbol of peace and rebirth with Noah after the flood destroyed the earth. Throughout the Bible, the dove is used as a form of sacrifice. In the New Testament, the Spirit bears fruit.

Goal

Recognize the dove as a sign of the Holy Spirit.

Bible Texts

Old Testament: Genesis 8:6-12, Psalm 55:6, Leviticus 1:14
New Testament: John 1:32, Matthew 3:16-17, Galatians 5:22

Verse to Learn

And when Jesus had been baptized, just as he came up from the water, suddenly the heavens were opened to him and he saw the Spirit of God descending like a dove and alighting on him. And a voice from heaven said, "This is my Son, the Beloved, with whom I am well pleased." Matthew 3:16-17

A Children's Message

Have you ever tried to talk with birds? Try it sometime and see if they will sing back to you. Do you know what a cardinal sounds like? If you call to a cardinal in a tree, it will think you are talking with it and will sing back to your call. Do you know what the dove's call sounds like? It's a very sad sound: coo-coo-coo, almost like a person crying. That is why it is called a mourning dove. The human voice, when it is very sad, sounds like the mourning dove's call.

Probably the most famous dove in history was the one Noah sent out from the ark after the flooding rains had stopped, to look for a place to land. When Noah first sent the dove to search for dry land, the dove returned to the ark because everything was still covered with water and it couldn't find a place to land. The second time Noah sent the dove out it came back with an olive branch in its beak. The branch meant that the dove had found dry ground and something alive; the flood was over. The third time Noah sent the dove out it didn't come back to the ark, which meant that it had found a place to nest. There was land ahead. Since then the dove and its olive branch have symbolized peace: you can find that symbol on stamps, stop-the-war symbols, and calls for peace throughout the world.

Another important dove in the Bible appears right after John baptizes Jesus. When Jesus comes out of the water, the heavens open up and the Spirit of God descends like a dove on Jesus. It is as though the Holy Spirit hovers over Jesus and spreads its wings of peace over him. Jesus tells us that the Holy Spirit hovers over us, too. So we are also filled with the Holy Spirit and with peace.

We know that God is all around us. When we puzzle over difficult things, trying to figure them out, God's Spirit, the dove hovers over us. The dove delivered the news of peace to Noah, and the dove sent peace to surround Jesus at his baptism, and on the cross, too. The dove, the Holy Spirit, surrounds us with peace and love. Listen for the singing. Try calling to that dove. It will hear you and call back to you. Look for the dove hovering over you. Feel it. Open your heart to that dove, the Holy Spirit, and you will be surrounded by peace and love.

Pray with the Children
Come, Holy Spirit, heavenly dove, kindle a flame of sacred love. Come, Holy Spirit, heavenly dove, model it on our Savior's love. Amen

Related Music
"Come, Holy Ghost, Our Souls Inspire," John B. Dykes
"Spirit of God, Descend upon My Heart," Frederick Atkinson
"Down to Earth, as a Dove," *Piae Cantiones*

To Do Together
Outside, listen for bird songs, especially the cooing song of the dove. Try imitating the dove's sound. Draw a picture of a dove in a tree or on top of a Christmas tree.

Epiphany 3

Symbol/Motif: gifts

Object: boxes with gold, frankincense, myrrh inside

The Wise Men, as well as the gifts they brought, represent the journey and the offerings we make to Jesus Christ. The gifts also remind us of love we receive from and give to God. Gold, durable and permanent, represents riches, power, and truth. Frankincense, a resin from balsam trees, represents our obedience to god. Myrrh represents our love to the Christ child and the love he brought to the world.

Goal
Understand what gold, frankincense, and myrrh represent.

Bible Texts
Old Testament: Psalm 72:11
New Testament: Matthew 2:1-12

Verse to Learn
Let the words of my mouth and the meditation of my heart be acceptable to you, O Lord, my rock and my redeemer. Psalm 19:14

A Children's Message
Giving a gift to a baby is so much fun. You can give a new blanket or hat. You could give a board book, soft toy, or a rattle to shake. There are so many possibilities; it is hard to decide what to give.

Imagine being a wise man going on a trip to give a birthday present to little Jesus. What gift would you choose to give to him? Choosing would be really hard because you wouldn't know what he needs. A blanket? A book? A rattle? What if that little child was a king? What on earth would you give to this little king?

The three Wise Men had to travel a hundreds of miles to find little Jesus. They didn't use a map or GPS; they followed a star. They did not know who or where this king was, except that he was an important king and that a star would lead them to him. They were kings themselves, so they knew what kings liked and wanted. They each brought a gift fit for a king. One of them brought gold because kings and queens wear crowns made of gold. Gold is a precious metal, difficult to find and expensive. That would be a great gift idea. Another wise man brought frankincense, which is something that burns to create a beautiful smell. It was a gift that showed respect and was used for worship. The third wise man brought myrrh, a perfumed oil to anoint the head of a king. Gold, frankincense, and myrrh. Three gifts definitely fit for a king.

We are not kings, we're not rich, and most of the time we're not that wise. What gifts can we bring? Do you think that Jesus will accept our gifts even if we are not rich, wise, or kings? If we want to be like the Wise Men and bring Jesus a gift, we just need to decide to do it and go. We don't need to worry about shopping for a present, because the only gift Jesus wants for his birthday is our hearts. We need to prepare our hearts so that they are given with love. Now that's a beautiful birthday present for our King!

Pray with Children

Dear God, help us to seek and follow the star that you shine for us. On our journey, teach us to be truthful and obedient with loving hearts worthy to be gifts to you. Amen

Related Music

"We Three Kings of Orient Are," J. H. Hopkins
"In the Bleak Midwinter," Gustavt T. Holst
"My Faith Looks Up to Thee," Lowell Mason

To Do Together

Design a box to hold a gift that you would like to give to Jesus. Decide the color it will be and the decorations it will have. Cover it with jewels. Find an object to represent your heart and decide where you will bring your gift.

Epiphany 4

Symbol/Motif: heart

Object: three boxes wrapped differently

The heart is a symbol of one person's love and devotion to another person, to God, to a group of people, or to an idea. The Bible refers to the heart as the inner being of our bodies: a person's thinking, feeling, and desiring. The Bible also says the human heart is the source of one's emotions, as well as the center that sets one's course of action. See Psalm 111:1, Proverbs 17:22, Matthew 11:29, and 2 Corinthians 3:3.

Goal

Recognize the planning, preparation, and praise involved in giving our hearts to God.

Bible Texts

Old Testament: Jeremiah 31:33, Psalm 139:23-24
New Testament: Ephesians 5:15-20

Verse to Learn

Search me, O God, and know my heart; test me and know my thoughts. See if there is any wicked way in me, and lead me in the way everlasting. Psalm 139:23-24

A Children's Message

Here are three boxes: different shapes, different sizes, with different wrapping paper. Can you guess what is inside any of them? Do the sizes give you any clues? How about the wrapping paper? If you were giving one of these boxes as a gift to someone, which one would you choose? If you were going to receive one of these, which one would you choose?

One of these gifts might be a "white elephant"! That's a gift that is kind of a joke—something that no one really wants. A beautiful box might have a white elephant inside, and a poorly wrapped box might have a treasure inside. You see the outside, but you can't see what's inside. Be careful, looks aren't everything, you know.

At Christmas, we receive the gift of Jesus. At Epiphany, the Wise Men give their gifts to Jesus. During the season of Epiphany, God gives us other gifts, like the gift of the Holy Spirit. Epiphany is the season when we celebrate the life of God's Son, Jesus, and celebrate the life we have as children of God—his gift of everlasting life. These are Epiphany gifts! Now it is our turn to give a gift—to Jesus, the one who gave everything for us. What could he possible want from us? The song says, "What can I give him, poor as I am? If I were a shepherd, I would bring a lamb. If I were a wise man, I would do my part. Yet what I can I give him? Give him my heart." The only thing we can give and the only thing Jesus wants is our hearts, our love.

If we're going to give our hearts and the love they represent, we need to prepare them, inside and out. Make them strong and loving, clean and beautiful. But wait—Jesus did all of that for us! His valentine for us is a cross. Why not make your heart a valentine to Jesus? Give your heart to him with love and no strings attached: now and forever.

Pray with Children

Dear God, teach us to prepare our hearts for you. Make them pure enough to give to you. Then take them and use them, for they are your own. Amen

Related Music

"Come, Thou Fount of Every Blessing," Robert Robinson

"Take My Life and Let It Be," Henri A. C. Malan

"We Give Thee But Thine Own," Mason and Webb *(Cantica Laudis)*

To Do Together

Use brightly colored paper, fabric, lace, and ribbon to create beautiful hearts. Hang them in prominent places throughout the house or present them to people you love.

Epiphany 5

Symbol/Motif: shell

Object: a seashell or a pearl

The shell is a product of the sea. It is the home of an animal that lives in the water. Many shells are beautiful. Some shells produce pearls, which are precious stones. In Christian art, John the Baptist is sometimes shown baptizing Jesus with water from a shell. The shell has become a symbol for Jesus' baptism and the baptism of God's children.

Goal

Understand that the shell has become a symbol for baptism.

Bible Texts

Old Testament: Job 28:18, Psalm 42:1
New Testament: Matthew 13:45-46, Matthew 7:6, Revelation 21:21

Verse to Learn

The kingdom of heaven is like a merchant in search of fine pearls; on finding one pearl of great value, he went and sold all that he had and bought it. Matthew 13:45-46

A Children's Message

If you've ever been to the ocean, you know that the best time to go for a walk on the beach to look for shells is at low tide, when the water level goes way down. That's when there's a great big beach with lots of shells that washed up with the high tide and were left in the sand. They will disappear just as soon as the water comes up again. Some shells are rough and textured while others are worn down and smooth. All of them are beautiful reminders of what a beautiful place the ocean is and the beautiful things God has created in this world, on the earth and in the sea.

A few shells hold a pearl, a jewel of the sea. A pearl begins as a tiny piece of sand inside the shell of an oyster or mussel. The living oyster or mussel coats the sand with a substance that will protect the animal inside the shell. Coats are added over several years and the grain of sand grows and grows into something beautiful that people search for and will pay a lot of money for—a pearl. People all over the world have pearl rings and necklaces; they are precious jewels, and each is one of a kind. Can you imagine finding a tiny little shell with a pearl inside it in the great big sea? It would be like finding a needle in a haystack.

The Holy Land has mountains, desert, and bodies of water, too, like the Sea of Galilee, the Red Sea, and the Mediterranean Sea. Many Bible stories involved the sea: Moses separating the Red

Sea, Jonah living inside the whale in the sea, and Jesus calling disciples who were fishermen and lived and worked near the sea. All of those people must have known about pearls.

Mary, the mother of Jesus, is sometimes compared to a beautiful shell because she carried Jesus inside her like a precious pearl. Jesus was the most precious pearl in the world. Jesus said that we should be like people searching for the best pearls in the world, and our life journey may take us all over the earth and across the seas. When we find that greatest pearl in the world, we should sell everything we have and buy it. But we don't have to buy Jesus—God gave him to us and all people. He is free! Look and find him.

Pray with Children

Dear God, guide us in our search for you. Give us strength when we get tired. Encourage us and show us the way when we are lost. Teach us to love, praise, and thank you. Amen

Related Music

"Let All Things Now Living," Welsh folk melody
"When Peace Is Like a River," Philip Bliss

To Do Together

Look for shells wherever you can find them: at the seashore, in the grocery store, in museums, pictured and described in books and magazines, as well as on the Internet. Learn about them and the creatures that live inside them. Find out where the various types live. Try drawing them; and start a shell collection.

Epiphany 6

Symbol/Motif: snow

Object: a crocheted, lace, or cut-paper snowflake

Snow is mentioned rarely in the Bible. It doesn't fit the climate of the Holy Land, but occasionally it can be seen on the mountaintops there. During Bible times, snow was associated with transcendence and imagination and considered a force of nature. The whiteness of snow in the Bible is associated with cleanliness, as well as God's transcendent brightness, Jesus at the transfiguration, the angel at the resurrection, and Christ in revelation.

Goal
Trust that Jesus makes us as white, pure, and beautiful as snowflakes.

Bible Texts
Old Testament: Daniel 7:9, Psalm 51:7, Isaiah 55:10
New Testament: Matthew 28:3, Mark 9:3, Revelation 1:14

Verse to Learn
Though your sins are like scarlet, they shall be like snow; though they are red like crimson, they shall become like wool. Isaiah 1:18

A Children's Message
On a bright, sunny day after a snowstorm, it is so bright you can hardly open your eyes. You might feel like covering your eyes or putting on your sunglasses. Some of us know all about snow,

have had snow days from school, built snowmen, and think snowflakes make great Christmas decorations. But for others who live in climates near the equator, this wouldn't make sense at all.

In the Holy Land, where the Bible was written, snow is very rare. When Jesus entered Jerusalem on the donkey, the people waved their palm leaves. Palm trees need to have warm climates and lots of sunshine. When the Bible does mention snow, it often associates snow with brightness and whiteness. The angel at the empty tomb of Jesus was like lightning, a huge burst of light, and his garments were as white as snow. Jesus took the disciples up the mountain for his transfiguration, and before their eyes his clothing became radiant and white—like snow. Such dramatic events!

Jesus does something just as dramatic for us. He washes us whiter than snow. He will forgive our sins and we will feel as white as big, puffy clouds on a summer day or beautiful white snowflakes on a winter day. Our bodies will be bright and white; our hearts and our spirits will be pure and white. We will be saints, even though we are sinners. We can't fix ourselves, so he does it for us. Jesus makes us whiter than snow.

Pray with Children
Dear God, you wash us whiter than snow. You give us clean hearts. You renew our spirits and never leave us. Thank you for all of these things. Amen

Related Music
"Whiter Than Snow," William G. Fischer
"Christ, Whose Glory Fills the Skies," M. Williamson
"How Great Thou Art," Swedish folk melody

To Do Together
Using paper and scissors, make many different snowflakes. Tape them in windows, hang them from the ceiling or lights, or decorate a tree branch with snowflakes and little white lights. If there is snow outside, dress appropriately, and make snow angels in the snow.

Epiphany 7

Symbol/Motif: five-pointed star of Bethlehem

Object: stars with different numbers of points

The star is a symbol of divine guidance, as was shown in the journey of the Wise Men to Bethlehem. A star may also represent God, the creator of the universe, the ultimate, infinite, and powerful God. The five-pointed star hints at the shape of the human form, and so can remind us of the birth of Jesus. In fact, this five-pointed star is sometimes called the Star of Bethlehem.

Goal
Learn the significance and meaning of the five-point star.

Bible Texts
Old Testament: Numbers 24:17
New Testament: Matthew 2:2, Philippians 2:15

Verse to Learn
It is I, Jesus, who sent my angel to you with this testimony for the churches. I am the root and the descendant of David, the bright morning star. Revelation 22:16

A Children's Message
When we look at the stars in the sky we can't count the number of points each star has. But when we draw or cut out stars we can make them with four, nine, seven, or even twelve points!

People love to make stars. We make them with just about any number of points. They also come in all different kinds of materials. Here is one that is metal. It sparkles. Some are made of paper, and here's one that's made of cloth, like a quilt. Here is a beautiful one; it's lace. Someone crocheted this one by hand. Any of these can decorate a Christmas tree. There are probably as many different stars on earth as there are in the sky.

On a moonless night, away from the city lights, sometimes we can see millions of stars in the sky. People have always loved to look at the stars. Star experts are called astronomers, after the Greek word *astro*, which means star. The study of the stars and their placement is called astronomy. At the beginning of the Old Testament, we read that on the fourth day of creation God created three heavenly lights: the sun, the moon, and the stars. And God put all of the stars in their proper places all over the heavens to give light to the earth. At the beginning of the New Testament, we read about the three kings who saw a magnificent star in the sky and were told to follow it. These three Wise Men began a journey that ended up at the manger of Jesus, where they gave him their gifts of gold, frankincense, and myrrh.

We can be earthly astronomers and study the stars in our night skies. This five-pointed star is called the Star of Bethlehem; its shape is like a child, the child in Bethlehem, the baby Jesus. This star looks joyful and playful, as was the baby Jesus. This star looks like its arms are spread, as Jesus spread his arms out in love to us, and spread the gospel all over the world. This star has five points, and Jesus had five wounds ~~in his hands~~ when he died on the cross. This star shines so brightly that it can guide us, just as Jesus guides us. This star shows how powerful and majestic God is: God not only gave us the stars, he gave us his Son, Jesus. God created the stars and the whole universe. God's stars are limitless, like the grains of sand along the seashore. Countless.

The Old Testament predicted the coming of Jesus: "A star shall come out of Jacob" (Numbers 24:17). And the Wise Men said, "We observed his star at its rising, and have come to pay him homage" (Matthew 2:2). Jesus said, "I am . . . the bright morning Star" (Revelation 22:16). We need to follow him; he is the star. Let's not only study stars; let's be stars like Jesus, bright and shining.

Pray with Children

Dear God, may we be your stars on this earth. Brighten our hearts and illuminate us from within so we will shine lovingly in this world. Amen

Related Music
"Star of the East, O Bethlehem Star," Amanda Kennedy
"Rise Up, Shepherd, and Follow," African American spiritual
"O Morning Star, How Fair and Bright," P. Nicolai

To Do Together
Draw, cut, and color three-, four-, and five-pointed stars. Make a mobile of stars or hang them in the window. Bring a tree branch inside. Decorate it with the stars and little white lights to remind us of Christ's light and love.

Epiphany 8

Symbol/Motif: tools and toolbox

Object: a toolbox filled with tools

Tools are used throughout the Bible for building boats, temples, cities, towers, houses, fortresses, walls, and tombs. They are part of a picture of an industrious people with a sense of reliance on God and his plan. The Bible also refers to God as a builder—the master builder forming and shaping the creation. In his parables, Jesus refers to wise and foolish builders.

Goal

Know that, just as carpenters use tools for their job, Christians use tools to build and grow in faith.

Bible Texts

Old Testament: 2 Samuel 5:9-12, Psalm 102:25, Ecclesiastes 3:3, Isaiah 48:13
New Testament: Mark 6:1-6, Galatians 5:22

Verse to Learn

Concerning this house that you are building, if you will walk in my statutes, obey my ordinances, and keep all my commandments by walking in them, then I will establish my promise with you, which I made to your father David. I will dwell among the children of Israel, and will not forsake my people Israel. 1 Kings 6:12-13

A Children's Message

If we were carpenters and were going to build a house, we would need a toolbox filled with lots of tools. In order to fix or build something, you need many different kinds of tools. Most of the time, carpenters don't work alone. They have many people who help them along the way. For us to build a house, we first need a permit from the city, bankers to loan us the money, architects to design the house. Then cement workers pour a foundation, carpenters build the structure, electricians wire, plumbers plumb, and painters paint. Interior decorators choose colors for the inside; landscapers decorate the outside. Lots of people work together to make the entire house like a beautiful work of art. We just have to hope that each of those people is trained, knows what they're doing, and has the right tools. You need tools to build a house, but the people using the tools are even more important than the tools themselves.

Jesus was a carpenter. With God, he designed, created, and built the world. They were the first planners, the best ever. They were the best architects, the best designers, and the best builders imaginable. They poured a very strong foundation, and they used the best materials for their creation. They were also the bankers: God sent Jesus to pay for us. They really believed in their project, and they knew what they were doing. They continue to guide and maintain it along the way. God also created people, us, his children.

God loved the world so much that he gave us his only Son, Jesus, to save the world. God has a plan for each of us, too. We need to figure out what that plan is and what tools we will need to accomplish it. God will teach us where to find the tools and how to use them. What we do with them will depend on how well we listen to and learn from God. We'd better get to work.

Pray with Children
Dear God, give us the tools we need to know you. Give us the tools we need to love you, to serve you, and to praise you. Help us along the way so that we praise you. Amen

Related Music
"Precious Lord, Take My Hand," George Allen
"Take My Life and Let It Be," Henri A. C. Malan
"Spirit of God, Descend Upon My Heart," Frederick Atkinson
"Spirit of the Living God," Daniel Iverson

To Do Together
Explore the family toolbox or workbench to see what tools there are. Learn about each tool and how to use it safely. Build something with the tools. Compare these tools to the tools you need to be a child of God. Which tools are more important? What kind of a box can you put all of them in?

Epiphany 9

Symbol/Motif: world/earth

Object: a globe or map of the earth and a map of the heavens

The Bible refers to the world in a multitude of different contexts. It can refer to the soil on the earth, to the earth as a planet, to the universe, and to all of creation. It connotes time when it uses the concept of "a new world." Jesus refers to himself as the "light of the world." He is the emissary from above who comes to save the earth below, only to ascend above and later return.

Goal
Know that God created and is in charge of the universe, and that we are God's children.

Bible Texts
Old Testament: Genesis 1:1—2:3, Psalm 104, Isaiah 66:1
New Testament: Hebrews 1:10, Mark 8:36, Matthew 5:13

Verse to Learn
Let the heavens be glad, and let the earth rejoice;
let the sea roar, and all that fills it;
let the field exult, and everything in it.
Then shall all the trees of the forest sing for joy
before the LORD.
Psalm 96:11-13a

A Children's Message

I'll bet your mom has a calendar right next to the phone. We need to be organized because lots of things go on a calendar: birthday parties, dentist appointments, soccer games, piano lessons. A calendar organizes and reminds us of some little things and big things that are coming up, like Halloween or Christmas, graduations or play dates.

People didn't always have a calendar like we have. Ancient people had a lunar calendar; the word *lunar* comes from "moon." Their calendar year was determined by where the moon was in the sky, the shape it was, and how large or small it was. The moon was so reliable, so rhythmic, and so regular that people decided to use it to organize the year. There were twelve full moons each year. They could count on it. The moon was so important to them that whenever there was a full moon, they had a party! Every month they had a party!

We still base our calendar on the moon. If you look at your calendar at home, it will tell you every month when the moon is going to be full. The dates of many of our holidays are based upon the new moon. The date of Easter is not based on when the schools want to have spring vacation. No, Easter is always the first Sunday following the first full moon after the first day of spring. The position and size of the moon is important in our calendars, too. Maybe we should have a party to celebrate every new moon!

The moon is a special creation of God. He gave the moon the responsibility to rule the night skies: to light a path at night. The sun and moon are the beautiful, bright, light handiworks of God's creation. The moon is so important and so reliable and so permanent that it has come to represent God's love and faithfulness to us.

We sing a song about the moon. It sounds like this:
I see the moon, and the moon sees me, down through leaves of the old oak tree.
Please let the light that shines on me, shine on the one I love.

God loves us and he shines his light and love on us. He provides us light for our feet to show us the way when it is dark in our lives or dark in our hearts. His light and love should fill our calendars and our lives. Look on your calendars to see when the moon will be full next. Be sure to thank God for that moon, his light, his love, his whole creation. We would be lost without it.

Pray with Children

Dear God, creator of the universe, let us praise you from all corners of the earth! Kings and workers, men and women, young and old—let all praise your name. Everything that has breath, praise your name! Amen

Related Music

"This Is My Father's World," M. D. Babcock
"He's Got the Whole World in His Hands," African American spiritual
"The Heavens Declare Your Glory," J. S. Bach

To Do Together

How many different kinds of globes and maps can you locate? Look for those that show the earth, oceans, and space. As you hunt, consider God's amazing role as the creator of it all, in fact, of the whole universe.

Season
of Lent

Season of Lent

About the Time
Six Sundays including Palm Sunday and 40 weekdays from Ash Wednesday to Easter Eve.

Seasonal Color
Purple, and black on Good Friday

Lent Themes
Time for personal reflection and preparation
Time for repentance, penitence, and sacrifice
God the Father, King of love and light of the world
God the Son, Lord of forgiveness and hope
God the Son, giver of life, Savior of God's people and the world

About the Season

Much as Advent is a time of preparation for Jesus' birth, so Lent is a time of preparation for Jesus' death and resurrection. Obviously, the tone of Lent is considerably more somber with its emphasis on penitence. Ash Wednesday is the first day of Lent. The name comes from the custom of placing ashes on the foreheads of those people who confess their sins. In the past, they would also have been dressed in sackcloth. Today, many churches place ashes on the foreheads of Ash Wednesday worshipers who wish to publicly confess their sins.

The season of Lent is named for the lengthening of daylight, and it recalls the 40 days Jesus spent in personal reflection after his baptism in the Jordan River. In the early church, Lent was a time of preparation for anyone who wished to be baptized.

During Lent, Christians spend time in self-reflection and penitence for their wrongdoings and sinful ways. Many Christians choose to give up something important to them for Lent, a practice that commemorates Jesus' fasting in the wilderness and the ultimate sacrifice he made on Good Friday. Lent is a time when Christians examine their personal lives, their spirituality, and their beliefs.

Lent is also a time when Christians can learn about the Christian faith, as their self-reflection turns them away from earthly things toward a search for knowledge and understanding of the nature of God. Lent should place Christians in a state of readiness for the death and resurrection of Jesus.

Holy Week

The final week of Christ's life on earth is known as Holy Week or Passion Week. The passion, from the Latin *patio* "to suffer or endure," consists of the events that occur from Palm Sunday through Easter Eve.

Palm Sunday

Palm Sunday commemorates the triumphal entry of Jesus into Jerusalem. This celebration has occurred in the church since the fourth century. Ceremonies include the blessing of palms and a procession representing the triumphant entry of Jesus.

Monday of Holy Week

Jesus drives the merchants out of the temple area and proclaims God's house to be a house of prayer. (Luke 19:45-46)

Tuesday of Holy Week

Jesus declares that people should give to the state what belongs to the state and to God what belongs to God. (Mark 12:14-17)

Wednesday of Holy Week

Jesus is anointed at Bethany. (Mark 14:3-9)

Maundy Thursday

Jesus washes the feet of the disciples (John 13:4-5); the Last Supper, where the blood seals God's covenant (Mark 14:22-25); Jesus prays in Gethsemane (Mark 14:32); Judas betrays Jesus and Jesus is arrested (Mark 14:44-46); Peter denies knowing Jesus. (Luke 22:54-62)

Good Friday

Jesus is brought before Pilate (Luke 23:1-4); Jesus is sentenced to death (Luke 23:18-25); Jesus is crucified (Luke 23:33-34); Jesus is buried. (Matthew 27:57-60)

Easter Eve

Pilate orders the tomb of Jesus to be carefully guarded (Matthew 27:62-66). This was the Sabbath day; hence Jews were not allowed to work. Since the second century, some churches have kept a vigil through Saturday night with Bible readings, meditative music, ringing of church bells, communion services, and even baptisms.

Key Bible Texts

Old Testament: Zechariah 9:9
New Testament: John 12:12-16

Lent for Children

Lent and Holy Week is a time for us to explore the core beliefs of the Christian faith and reflect on our relationship with God, the church, each other, and ourselves. The dramatic events of Jesus' final days are central to our understanding of who he is, and what he did for us.

Lent 1

Symbol/Motif: coins

Object: a snack-size bag filled with coins, a grocery bag filled with objects of value, a trash bag holding scraps of paper with words written on them, and a cross

Coins suggest riches, abundance, and wealth; but they can also make us think of greed and betrayal. In the Old Testament, the brothers of Joseph sell him for twenty pieces of silver. During Lent, the coin reference is to Judas's betrayal of Jesus for thirty pieces of silver: Judas sold his love of God for money. God warns his people not to become ensnared by riches, but to give to God what is God's.

Goal

Recognize that coins represent money, greed, and betrayal.

Bible Texts

Old Testament: Proverbs 8:17-21, Exodus 20:23
New Testament: Matthew 26:14-15, Luke 22:3-6

Verse to Learn

But strive first for the kingdom of God and his righteousness, and all these things will be given to you as well. Matthew 6:33

A Children's Message

Here are three bags holding different things. The first one has many coins; it is worth lots of money. The second one is filled with things that money can buy, like a car, a house, a book, a ring, a golf ball, a boat. The third bag has just a few scraps of paper. The coins in the first bag will buy some of the things in the second bag. But some of the things in the second bag require many more coins than you have in this first bag. People spend their entire lives trying to fill up this first bag so that they will have enough coins to buy all of the things in the second bag. In fact, lots of people want this second bag to be much larger than it is. Sometimes they won't have enough coins to buy all of the things they want to be in that bag. Lots of people have more things in this middle bag than they can afford or have paid for. Some people are never happy because they never have enough coins in this first bag to buy all of the things they want.

The third bag is the biggest but weighs the least. It feels empty but is filled with the most important things—things money can't buy. This one says "happiness." Can you buy happiness? This one says "goodness." Can you pay someone to make you a good person? "Life." Can you buy it? "Loyalty." Can you pay someone to be loyal to you? "Forgiveness." If you do something really bad to someone, can you pay that person to forgive you? "Friendship." Can you buy a friend?

"Love." Can you buy love? Here is a cross. No matter how many coins you have, you cannot buy that. It's okay because that is free. Jesus, our Savior, gives it to us.

God wants us to work just as hard at finding the things in this third bag as we do at filling the other bags. God says that if we seek him first we will find those things and also come to know God. God is the real treasure, not all of the things we see around us. Remember what is in this third bag, things that come from God: things like goodness, happiness, love, forgiveness, loyalty, and our Savior. If we love God, our lives will be full of something finer than silver and gold: Jesus.

Pray with Children
Dear God, our world is filled with things that may distract us in our mission to find you. Help us raise our eyes from earthly things to seek you and the kingdom of heaven. Amen

Related Music:
"Seek Ye First the Kingdom of God," Karen Lafferty
"Trust and Obey," D. B. Towner
"Take Time to Be Holy," W. D. Longstaff

To Do Together
Find or make a beautiful bag. Fill it with things that remind you of what God loves. Include things that can't be bought. Write a letter to Jesus thanking him for giving his life for us and add it to the bag.

Lent 2

Symbol/Motif: Passion crosses

Object: two pieces of wood with pointed ends

In the ancient world, the cross represented a cruel, painful death, a crucifixion. The victim was tied to an upright piece of wood, sometimes with a crossbeam in the middle or near the top. A crossbeam with pointed ends, like the one on a Passion cross, reminds us of Jesus nailed to the cross on Good Friday. This cross also reminds us of our complete reconciliation through his death.

Goal
Learn that the Passion cross represents the crucifixion story.

Bible Texts
Old Testament: Isaiah 53:3-9
New Testament: John 19:10-22, Matthew 16:24, Luke 9:23, John 3:14

Verse to Learn
Even though I walk through the darkest valley, I fear no evil; for you are with me; your rod and your staff—they comfort me. Psalm 23:4

A Children's Message
On these two pieces of wood there are four points altogether—from side to side and top to bottom. The piece of wood going up and down on a cross is called the post; the horizontal piece

of wood is called a crossbeam. The crossbeam can be placed anywhere on that post—near the top or the bottom, or anywhere in between. However the horizontal piece of wood is connected with the post, together they become a cross. It is a symbol that is known throughout the world. Throughout history, people who were identified as criminals were sometimes executed on a cross; that kind of death is called a crucifixion. Jesus was crucified on a cross because the Romans and some of his own people thought he wanted to overthrow the government.

People have named over four hundred different kinds of crosses, each with a different shape and placement of the crossbeam on the post. One familiar cross we see today is called the Latin cross. It places the crossbeam a third of the way down the post. No matter what shape crosses have, each one represents Jesus. Roman Catholics usually show Jesus on the cross, and Protestants usually display an empty cross. Believers may make a sign of the cross with their hands in front of their bodies when they pray or when they see a cross, as a way to remember the death and sacrifice of Jesus.

These pieces of wood have pointed ends. The points are meant to look like nails because Jesus was nailed to the cross. This passion cross represents the suffering and crucifixion of Jesus during Holy Week. The shape of the cross might remind you of the body of Jesus, with his head and his feet on the post, and his arms on the crossbeam. Pilate demanded that the four letters "INRI" be placed on Jesus' cross. These Latin letters are the initials for "Jesus of Nazareth, King of the Jews." The points of this post aim up and down, into the depths of the earth and up to the heavens. Or we can think of the post pointing north and south like the crossbeam points from east to west so that they form a circle around the earth. The sacrifice of Jesus encompasses the world and includes everyone in it. Jesus isn't left on that cross. This passion cross reminds us that Jesus died and rose to conquer death. He gives us hope and life and love forever.

Pray with Children

Dear Jesus, help us appreciate and understand your suffering as we stand beneath your cross. Help us to thank you, praise you, and honor you for your sacrifice. Amen

Related Music

"Beneath the Cross of Jesus," Frederick Maker

"Ah, Holy Jesus," Johann Crüger

"When I Survey the Wondrous Cross," Isaac Watts

To Do Together

Make a cross of nails by placing two or three nails together vertically and two or three nails together horizontally with the points of the nails inside. Wrap thin wire around the nails where they touch in the center. Hang a string or chain around the cross so that it can be worn as a necklace, or hung on a tree, on a wall, or from a window.

Lent 3

Symbol/Motif: crown of thorns

Object: three crowns: one of jewels, one of flowers, one of nails

In the Bible, people who wear crowns represent royalty, power, or honor; crowns also are rewards for God's children who do good works. But sometimes crowns cause fighting, war, and defeat and God warns that a crown is not secure for all generations, and riches do not endure forever. Jesus set aside his crown of honor for a crown of thorns when he accepted all of our sins and died for our atonement.

Goal
Explore how the crown of thorns represents the suffering and mockery Jesus experienced.

Bible Texts
Old Testament: Psalm 103:1-5, Psalm 21:3, Isaiah 62:3
New Testament: Matthew 27:29

Verse to Learn
You are worthy, our Lord and God, to receive glory and honor and power, for you created all things. Revelation 4:11a

A Children's Message
When you play dress-up, you might wear something on your head: a fancy hat of your grandma's, a firefighter's helmet, a painter's beret, or a baseball cap. Even when you don't have any other part of a costume on, hats or helmets can show right away what you are pretending to be.

Place a football helmet on your head and you are a sports star. Put a veil on your head, and you become a bride. With a wreath of roses on your head you might be a nymph celebrating spring. Wear a gold crown filled with jewels; you would be a king or a queen.

Jesus didn't actually wear a crown, but he was a real king. People didn't understand him or believe him. Many thought he was lying, or making fun, or just pretending. Some thought that when he said he was the Son of God, he was swearing against God. Because of that, he was whipped and mocked and made to wear a crown of prickly thorns. It wasn't beautiful and soft with fur or lace or flowers, and it wasn't covered with precious stones. No, it was hard and sharp. And it didn't just sit on his head, but it dug into his skin and cut him so that he bled. Jesus didn't look much like a king then. He looked more like a prisoner, with his hands tied behind him, stripped of his clothes, and with thorns in his head. He looked to be the lowest of the low, as far from royalty with a jeweled crown, a velvet robe, and a gold throne as he could be.

Do you know the saying, "Sticks and stones will break my bones, but words will never hurt me"? Sometimes words can hurt you just as much as sticks, stones, and nails. Words can make you feel terrible; you can't see it on the outside, but words can hurt your insides. People hurt Jesus on the inside and the outside. Some of them pretended to worship him, kneeling down in front of him; but they were just mocking him. They even spit on him. On the cross, Jesus took all of the bad things people did the entire history of the world, and he said, "Forgive them." He died for us. His crown of thorns became even greater than a royal crown; it became a divine crown. His throne is not just golden; it's heavenly. Let's thank him for that.

Pray with Children
Holy Jesus, you have given us everything. Help us to focus on your patience, your pain, and your promise. Thank you for your sacrifice and love for us. Amen

Related Music
"Crown Him with Many Crowns," George Elvey
"O Lamb of God Most Holy," Nikolaus Decius
"Ah, Dearest Jesus," Johann Crüger

To Do Together
Make a wreath of grapevines, pinecones, or leaves, and decorate it with lace, flowers, nuts, and thorns from the garden. Discuss how each part of the wreath looks and feels, and what they could represent.

Lent 4

Symbol/Motif: garments

Object: a robe of many colors

The vesting, investing, and divesting of garments occur frequently in the Bible. The significance is physical, social, economic, religious, moral, or spiritual. These garments are earned, given, or taken away; they are protective, for display, or symbolic of larger ideas. Garments can be festive, mournful, deceitful, royal, and ceremonial; or they can show poverty. The imagery in the garments of Jesus reflects his purpose, his human and divine being.

Goal
Discover the importance of garments in the Bible stories from Joseph to Jesus.

Bible Texts
Old Testament: Isaiah 63:1-6, Psalm 21:3, Isaiah 62:3
New Testament: John 19:23, Matthew 27:28-29

Verse to Learn
If you conquer, you will be clothed like them in white robes, and I will not blot your name out of the book of life. Revelation 3:5a

A Children's Message

You can tell a cowboy by looking at his clothes. You can spot a firefighter or a police officer in a crowd. Clothes might give you a clue about where and when someone lived. Clothes often tell whether someone is rich or poor, a priest or a prisoner, an astronaut or a bride. Our clothes tell others what we have, who we are, and what we are.

Joseph's father had many children, but he loved Joseph more than any other. He gave only Joseph a bright, beautiful coat with every color of the rainbow. Because Jacob loved Joseph more than his any of his brothers, they hated him. They ripped Joseph's special coat and stripped it off him, and then threw him in a pit. When a trader came along, the brothers sold him for twenty pieces of silver. Because of a coat, Joseph went from being loved to the being hated. Later he became a top advisor to the king of Egypt and once again wore beautiful garments.

Jesus, too, wore different garments. His first garments were swaddling clothes in the manger. He wore the work clothes of a carpenter, and later when he traveled around teaching and healing people, some of them thought his garments were miraculous and wanted to touch them. Jesus' enemies tore his clothes from him and covered him with fake scarlet royal garments to mock and laugh at him before they hung him on a cross.

Our garments tell something about us, too. They reflect who we are, where we're going, what colors we like, and how fast we're growing. Do those things matter to God? No. God tells us not to wish for clothes or other things we don't have. God tells us not to value what is on the outside of our bodies, but to decorate our insides with love. Our inside jewels might be a loving and gentle heart, a quiet spirit, a beautiful mind before God. With those garments, we will be robed with colors of righteousness. Then we can say, "My whole being shall exult in my God; for he has clothed me with the garments of salvation, he has covered me with the robe of righteousness" (Isaiah 61:10). Let us be God's beautiful children, clothed with garments of love and righteousness and worthy of God's favorite kingdom.

Pray with Children

Dear God, may the "inside garments" show our love and praise for you. Clothe us with gentle spirits, loving hearts, and beautiful robes of righteousness. We thank you in Jesus' name. Amen

Related Music

"Were You There," African American spiritual

"What Wondrous Love Is This," Walker's Southern harmony

To Do Together

Find a variety of pieces of fabric, such as burlap, velvet, satin, a multicolored sheet, a white sheet, black fabric, gold-colored rope, and a fancy purse with silver coins. Use the fabric and props as costumes as you re-enact Bible stories.

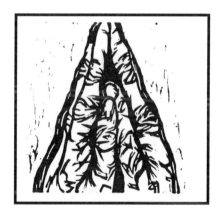

Lent 5

Symbol/Motif: hands

Object: hands

The Bible has almost two thousand references to the hand as part of the body or an extension of the arm. Some of the references are literal and some are figurative. The right hand sometimes connotes favor and power, the left hand sometimes connotes disfavor and rejection. Hands do many things for many different purposes: perform tasks, give power and authority, take control, specify a location, and express people's wishes.

Goal

Show the use of hands in praying to God.

Bible Texts

Old Testament: 2 Kings 10:15, Psalm 17:7, Psalm 63:4, Isaiah 49:16
New Testament: Matthew 22:44, Luke 4:40

Verse to Learn

Because your steadfast love is better than life, my lips will praise you. So I will bless you as long as I live; I will lift up my hands and call on your name. Psalm 63:3-4

A Children's Message

If I ask you to fold your hands and close your eyes, what am I asking you to do? Whether we pray alone or with other people, we usually fold our hands. Or we might hold our open hands together, palm to palm. Sometimes we pray holding hands with other people around a table or to form a circle.

If the crossing guard holds her hand to traffic, what does she want the traffic to do? If someone asks you to put your hand on the Bible, what are you asked to do? If a baby reaches his hands up to you, what does he want you to do? If I wring my hands like this, what am I doing? If someone cups his hands together, turns them over and extends them, he is often asking another person to give him something.

When I hold my hand out to you like this, I am telling you that I want to shake your hand. Is that a friendly gesture? If I cover my face with my hands, what do you think I am feeling? Some people, especially those who can't hear, communicate with their hands using sign language. You will know what I mean if I raise my hand to "give you five." If we clap our hands loudly what are we showing? A potter shapes a pot with her hands. A minister holds his hands above us before we leave church; what is he doing? If I gently and warmly place my hands on your face or throw you a kiss, what am I showing you? Hands can express love, warmth, and support, but they can also show fear, anger, and sadness.

Many times when we read about God in the Bible, there is a reference to God's hands. Moses said to God, "Your right hand, O LORD, glorious in power—your right hand, O LORD, shattered the enemy" (Exodus 15:6). God's hands are powerful: they can heal and they can hurt. We can feel God's hands on us and all around us. This week, gently lay your hands on the people around you. Hold hands with someone who is afraid. Your hands can be helping hands. You can clap your hands in joy, raise your hands in praise to God, gently touch others' hands in love, and fold your hands in quiet prayer to God. Your hands can show what is in your heart.

Pray with Children
Dear God, we thank you for hands, including ours. We thank you also for the big and little things your hands have done for us. Teach us to use our hands in loving ways for others, and to fold them in praise and prayer to you. Amen

Related Music
"Take My Life and Let It Be," Henri A. C. Malan
"Oh, Be Careful Little Hands What You Do!" old melody
"Savior, Like a Shepherd Lead Us," William B. Bradbury

To Do Together
Before meals this week (or before going to bed), ask the members of your family to hold hands together and raise them in praise to God as you offer a prayer of thanksgiving.

Lent 6—Passion/ Palm Sunday

Symbol/Motif: palm leaves

Object: palm leaves

The palm tree is tall and regal. It has leaves only at the top that look like they are bursting forth. It produces fruit to eat and sap for drinking. Its roots grow deep because they are seeking water. Palm trees only grow in certain geographic locations; they need water and a moderate climate. They are associated with fertile tropical lands and with oases in the desert. Palm leaves paved Jesus' route into Jerusalem before his crucifixion.

Goal
Spread palm leaves to praise Christ the King.

Bible Texts
Old Testament: Exodus 15:27, Psalm 92:12, Isaiah 9:14
New Testament: Luke 19:28-40, John 12:12-13, Matthew 21:1-11

Verse to Learn
Blessed is the king who comes in the name of the Lord! Peace in heaven, and glory in the highest heaven! Luke 19:38

A Children's Message

Do palm trees grow on your street? If you live in Florida or Arizona, that would be a pretty silly question because palm trees are all over the place. But if you live in Maine, you may never have seen a palm tree. Why? Palm trees don't grow there because it gets too cold in the wintertime.

A palm tree grows very tall and stately. Its long, slender trunk has leaves only at the very top; they burst into the sky almost like fireworks. The land of the Bible had the right balmy, warm climate for palm trees, and they were a welcome sight to many people as they traveled. Palm trees and their leaves were very important where Jesus lived, and they were used in festivals. Look around; today we have many palm fronds in our church. The people in the Bible times thought the leaves of the palm tree were like arches, so when they were victorious in battle, they carried palm leaves to celebrate and treat the winners as kings. When Jesus entered Jerusalem, they spread palm leaves out in front of him as though he were a king.

The palm tree almost looks like a person with feet firmly planted in the ground, arms and hands stretched up to the sky. The Bible actually compares a person to a palm tree: "The righteous flourish like the palm tree" (Psalm 92:12). The palm leaves in our church today are used to help us celebrate Jesus' entry into Jerusalem, so we can welcome him just as the people of Jerusalem did long ago. On Sunday Jesus comes into the city like a king, but many things change as the week goes on. On Friday he is crucified on the cross.

The palm tree is not like a maple or oak tree, whose leaves change to yellow or red or brown in the fall. It is like an evergreen tree that is green all year long. The palm tree can remind us of Jesus, who has roots on earth and is tall and kingly, with leaves bursting out and reaching to heaven, where he prepares a place for us. Jesus is like the Tree of Life, giving us life everlasting. If we place three palm leaves together, we have one for Jesus, God the Son; one for God the Father; and one for God the Holy Spirit: three in one. We need to spread our leaves out for Jesus and thank him for preparing our way.

Pray with Children

Dear Jesus, we thank you for your humble yet royal ride on the donkey into Jerusalem. May we grow like palm trees in a desert oasis, praising you as our Savior, Lord, and King of the world. Amen

Related Music

"Hosanna, Loud Hosanna," J. Threlfall/Herzogl

"Ride On! Ride On in Majesty," H. H. Milman/John B. Dykes

To Do Together

Take a field trip to a botanical garden or search the Internet or an encyclopedia to learn about different kinds of palm trees. Look carefully at the trunk, leaves, and fruit of the palm trees. Draw diagrams and pictures of different kinds palm trees. Check a globe or map and find where palm trees grow.

Season of Easter

Season of Easter

About the Time
Easter Day, five Sundays and Ascension Sunday, or 50 days; Easter begins on Easter Day and continues for 50 days, leading up to Pentecost Sunday

Seasonal Color
White and gold

Easter Themes
Jesus' resurrection
God the creator, giver of life and love
God the Son, sacrifice and Savior of the world
God's people, saved and transformed

About the Season

Easter is a season of joy and triumph, when life is victorious over death. It is a time to celebrate the birth, life, death, and resurrection of Jesus. Easter is the "Queen of the Festivals" of the church year, the day on which we commemorate the resurrection of our Lord. For the early church, the celebration was associated with the Jewish Passover. Throughout the non-English-speaking world, this is known as *pascha*, the Latin word for Passover (Hebrew *pesah*).

The date on which Easter falls varies from year to year because it is determined by the rotation of the moon. Easter falls on the first Sunday after the first full moon after the vernal equinox (March 21). That will also determine the date for Ash Wednesday and the beginning of Lent. The date of Easter, which determines much of the rest of the church calendar, is fixed according to the Paschal Calendar developed by the monk Dionysius Exiguus in A.D. 527. Fixing Easter in this manner causes it to fall at the same time as the Jewish Passover, since the first Easter coincided with that feast.

The word *Easter* evolved from the name Eostres, the name of an Anglo-Saxon goddess of spring who was honored at the vernal equinox. Easter was originally celebrated as one continuous festival, but in the fourth century it was divided into separate observances of the Resurrection, the Ascension, and Pentecost. Because Christ rose from the dead, Easter Sunday is also called Resurrection Sunday, the most joyful day of the Christian year. The liturgical colors used during the Easter Season are white and gold, signifying purity, royalty, and joy.

Though every Sunday is considered to be a "little Easter," the season of Easter is made up of the five Sundays following Easter Sunday, leading up to Ascension Day, usually observed on the fortieth day after Easter. In some Christian communities, Easter is associated with baptism, emphasizing the Christian's identification with and acceptance of Christ's resurrection.

The number three is the most frequently used number in the Bible; part of its significance derives from the three days between Good Friday and Easter, when Jesus was in the tomb. After three days, the triumphal resurrection on Easter morning becomes the victorious symbol of everlasting life. The Old Testament story of Jonah's three days inside the great fish foreshadows the three days Jesus was in the tomb. Jonah's experience signifies God's judgment, redemption, and salvation. To escape the call of God, Jonah sets out to sea, the very symbol of chaos and danger. After offering to be thrown into the sea to calm the storm, Jonah is swallowed by the great fish. He calls to God for help from "the depths of the grave." After three days and three nights, God "spoke to the fish, and it spewed Jonah out upon the dry land" (Jonah 2:10). Throughout the history of the church, this image has been used to depict our salvation from death through Christ's death and resurrection. The number three continues its significance and symbolism by representing the Holy Trinity.

Because of Easter's relationship to the lunar calendar, many popular seasonal traditions, such as Easter eggs and the Easter bunny are more closely associated with pagan rites of fertility and spring than with Easter. However, they are carried over into the Christian themes of transformation and traditions associated with birth and new life.

Key Bible Texts
Old Testament: Jonah 1:11–2:10
New Testament: Matthew 12:40

Easter for Children
Easter is the most celebrated holiday of the Christian year. It is a day and season of joy and triumph. Its message is that Christ is risen indeed, that death has no victory because the one true Life has overcome death.

Easter 1

Symbol/Motif: butterfly

Object: a picture of a butterfly, or one in a jar or mounted

The Bible tells the story of transformations: of the spirit, of the body, of the mind, and even of a nation. The human spirit grows and develops while on this earth, and human life is always changing. Metamorphosis is constantly taking place, sometimes because of our choices and often because of the will of God. The butterfly symbolizes the transformation of those in the world and the world itself.

Goal
Trust that Jesus' resurrection changes everything.

Bible Texts
Old Testament: Ecclesiastes 12:7, Psalm 32:1-5
New Testament: 1 Peter 2:10, 1 Corinthians 15:51-52, Galatians 1:23

Verse to Learn
So if anyone is in Christ, there is a new creation: everything old has passed away; see, everything has become new! 2 Corinthians 5:17

A Children's Message

Do you ever notice how things change? When we lose our baby teeth, new ones grow in. When our feet grow, we need new shoes. When spring comes, the brown grass turns green again. When water freezes, it turns to ice. And when ice warms up, it turns back to water. Rain changes to sunshine. Night turns to day. Sorrow and sadness turn to joy. Dark turns to light. We change from sad to happy, from young to old.

Some things change quickly and some changes take a long time. Some changes are manmade while others are part of the natural world. Some are studied carefully by scientists, but others happen without anyone noticing. The butterfly has the most dramatic and beautiful metamorphosis. It only takes a few months to go from a tiny egg, to a caterpillar, to a gorgeous butterfly and then to travel five thousand miles! Many insects are swatted or stepped on by people, but butterflies are collected and admired; they are even compared to angels. Human beings also experience a metamorphosis, one that's even more beautiful than the butterfly's. Our metamorphosis takes place over a long time: from a little egg into a newborn baby, from not being able to talk to graduating from college. It's the same as the butterfly: from an egg to an adult.

Another dramatic and beautiful metamorphosis took place in Jesus. His metamorphosis is from God to baby to man to Savior and back to God. He is the Creator, the Rescuer, and the Savior of the world. Our metamorphosis is almost as dramatic because we develop from a sinful person to a saved person to one with eternal life. That is what Easter is all about: the metamorphosis of sin to salvation. It's the most dramatic transformation, and it goes farther than the miles from north to south that the butterfly travels. Our change is from evil to good, from sinful to saved. Now that is a beautiful metamorphosis!

Pray with Children

Dear God, you created a bright and beautiful world filled with creatures large and small. Help us grow into beautiful creatures, ready and eager to give you praise. Amen

Related Music

"Let All Things Now Living," Welsh tune

"The Butterfly Song," Brian Howard

"All Things Bright and Beautiful," John Rutter

To Do Together

Search outside for a caterpillar. Place it in a jar along with grass and sticks. Watch its development. In the meantime, look up information on butterflies. You might read *Butterflies Fly* by Y. Winter, illustrated by K. Lloyd-Jones (Charlesbridge Press, 2000) or *Butterflies of the World, Fandex Family Field Guide* (Workman Publishing, 2002).

Easter 2

Symbol/Motif: crown

Object: a crown and a chair

In the Bible, crowns often represent royalty, honor, and blessing. However, sometimes crowns are the cause of fighting, war, and defeat. God warns that riches do not endure forever and that a crown is not secure for all generations. Blessings crown the righteous; and such crowns are also rewards for God's children who do good works. Jesus set aside his crown of honor for a crown of thorns when he took on all of our sins and died for our atonement.

Goal
Learn about the kingship and royalty of Christ.

Bible Texts
Old Testament: Psalm 21:3, Psalm 47:8, Proverbs 10:6, Isaiah 62:3
New Testament: Matthew 27:29, Hebrews 4:16, Revelation 20:11

Verse to Learn
Let us therefore approach the throne of grace with boldness, so that we may receive mercy and find grace to help in time of need. Hebrews 4:16

A Children's Message
What would you do if you were a queen or a king for a day? You could order anybody to do anything you wanted! You could have anything you wanted to eat. You could go anywhere you wanted to go. But . . . could you order someone to love you? Could you order someone to be nice to you? Could you order someone to give you a diploma? Could you pay someone to make you a doctor? Could you buy the medal at the swim meet? Could you be on the team without even trying out? Even if you were a queen or a king for the day, there are lots of things you wouldn't be able to do.

What would you *give* if you were royalty for a day? You could give food to everyone who needed it. You could send coats, sweatshirts, and blankets to anyone who was cold. You could give toys to children who didn't have any. You could even give money to someone who wanted to go to college. You can give someone love, but can you give someone happiness? You can give someone an idea, but can you make that person carry it out? A human queen can't make everyone happy. A human king can't make the world peaceful.

We are lucky because Jesus is a king of all humankind, an everlasting king; he is God's Son. Jesus is not only king for a day, but he is a king forever. He had the power to do it all for us, and he did! He had the power to come to earth and die for us, save us, and prepare a way and a place for us in heaven. If he had told us how to do those things, we couldn't have done them, so he did them for us.

Jesus has a royal crown on a divine throne. He shares it with the Father and the Holy Spirit. They will teach us things and will expect great things from us. They will even give us the will to want to do them. Our responsibility is to learn as much as we can, be listeners, be the best people we can be, and share our things with others. God's words sometimes seem far away and difficult to hear. But if we are quiet, prayerful, and sincere, we will hear them. Since Jesus is a king, we must also worship and praise him. He promises to teach us to be his loving children and do all of the things he wants us to do. Our job is to thank and honor him every day.

Pray with Children

Dear God, thank you for loving us as little children in your giant kingdom. Give us the courage to believe that you will save us, and grant us a place in your kingdom. Amen

Related Music

"Beautiful Savior, King of Creation," Silesian folk song
"All Hail the Power of Jesus' Name," Oliver Holden
"Jesus Loves Me," William Bradbury

To Do Together

Draw a picture of King Jesus with many different kinds of crowns and a throne. Include in the picture some of the things that Jesus has given us. Start with a heart, or something that reminds you of love.

Easter 3

Symbol/Motif: mother and child/heart/mother's love

Object: a heart or a mother/child figure

Throughout the Bible, motherhood is understood as the greatest blessing for women. The Bible defines a mother's responsibility to protect, nurture, and teach her children, physically and spiritually. Eve is identified as the mother of all and is told to bear children. Mary, the mother of Jesus, provides the most wonderful example of a woman who lives her life in response to God's love.

Goal
Appreciate that God's ultimate act of love teaches us how to love.

Bible Texts
Old Testament: Exodus 20:12, Psalm 131:2, Exodus 13:14, Genesis 1
New Testament: John 3:16, Luke 2:41–52, 1 Corinthians 13

Verse to Learn
Love is patient; love is kind; love is not envious or boastful or arrogant. It bears all things, believes all things, hopes all things, endures all things. 1 Corinthians 13:4, 7

A Children's Message
Before a baby learns to talk, to walk, to feed him or herself, she or he has already learned what it is to feel safe. A baby learns to trust that it will be fed, hugged, changed, sung to, and smiled

at. Trust in that care and safety depends in part on seeing the familiar faces of loving people, hearing familiar voices, and even feeling familiar heartbeats. The baby learns early on about community; the baby discovers that it is not alone, it has company—typically a mother.

We are lucky if we have felt the love that comes from a committed parent or caregiver who shares everything he or she has with a little baby. What comes from a such a person's heart cannot be created anywhere else in the world, cannot be bought anywhere in the world, cannot be found anywhere else in world. We are wealthy beyond words because of our parents.

If a general in the military has a lot of medals on his or her uniform, we know that he or she has done heroic deeds. Basketball teams win medals and are awarded championships. We don't do anything like that for our mothers. We don't give our fathers medals or call them champions. But because of them, we are honored. The Bible says, "Hear, my child, your father's instruction, and do not reject your mother's teaching; for they are a fair garland for your head, and pendants for your neck" (Proverbs 1:8-9). Because of your mother and father, you have your own crowns and jewels.

Wear those jewels. Love your parents completely and obediently. Follow the commandment to honor your father and your mother. God teaches us how to love, why to love, when to love. God so loved the world that he gave us his Son, Jesus Christ. As God loves us, and our parents love us, so we are to love our parents. That is an honor we can wear like the crown jewels!

Pray with Children

Dear God, take our possessions, our minds, and our wills. Take our hands, our feet, and our whole bodies. Take our lives and our love and use them to share your love with those around us. Amen

Related Music

"Jesus Loves Me," W. B. Bradbury
"Take My Life and Let It Be," Henri A. C. Malan
"Though I May Speak," English folk melody

To Do Together

Gather in a place with a good view of God's world: a park, a beach, or a backyard. Take turns naming things you love and are thankful for that start with the letters of the alphabet. The first person names something that starts with A. The next person repeats the A word and adds something that starts with B. Continue with the whole alphabet. There is a lot to be thankful for!

Easter 4

Symbol/Motif: lily

Object: three boxes wrapped with a manger, a cross, and a lily, each inside one box

Flowers, with their blooms and blossoms bursting forth in spring, symbolize love, beauty, purity, and holiness. Flowers represent the grace God showers upon his people. Flowers connote frailty, transience, growth, beauty, death, and decay of the natural world, corresponding to the lives and works of humankind on this earth. The righteous person is compared to the blossoming and flourishing of a flower. The lily, specifically the Easter lily, represents Christ's life, triumphant over death, which we celebrate Easter Sunday.

Goal

Recognize the lily as a symbol of the risen Lord.

Bible Texts
Old Testament: Isaiah 35:1, Psalm 103:15, Hosea 14:5
New Testament: Luke 12:27, Matthew 6:28-29

Verse to Learn
Consider the lilies of the field, how they grow; they neither toil nor spin, yet I tell you, even Solomon in all his glory was not clothed like one of these. Matthew 6:28-29

A Children's Message
We are surrounded by white in church this morning. We are sitting on a white blanket. The pastor has a white robe on this morning. There is a white banner. There are white flowers all around. White is color that represents purity, brightness, glory, and victory. The white Easter lily blossoms look like they are dancing, alive, joyous, and glorious. Let's find where the lilies are in this story.

Today is a holiday. As with all big holidays, we are going to celebrate this one with presents. Not just one present, but three. One is beautifully wrapped in gold—fit for a king. One is sorrowfully wrapped in black with a red bow. And one is gorgeously wrapped in white with a gold bow—that must be for someone special.

Let's open the first one to see what's inside. It's a manger with the baby Jesus. But, you say, that's for Christmas! A long time ago. Are we going to get Christmas gifts today? Let's put the manger on top of the box and open the next one. This bow is red and the paper is black. Last Friday was the darkest day of the year, yet we call it "Good" Friday because the thing we celebrated Friday was blood on a cross. On Christmas a baby was born. On Friday that child, now a man, died on a cross. We call it "good" because he died for us. Let's see what is in this package that is beautifully wrapped in white with a gold bow. On that first Easter morning when Mary went to find the body of her son, Jesus, the tomb was empty. Maybe this box is empty. Maybe there is nothing in it, just like the tomb. Let's see. Oh, it is a lily, an Easter lily. This lily shows us that Jesus rose from the dead and is alive. We have lots of lilies in the church today because we not only celebrate his life with the manger and his death with the cross. We also celebrate that empty tomb. This lily represents his life over death.

On Easter we receive the third of three important gifts Jesus gave us; you can't have one without the other. They all go together. Three wonderful presents: a baby in a manger; a cross with his blood shed for us; and today, an Easter lily, gloriously alive!

We are surrounded by white in church this morning. We sit on a beautiful white blanket. The pastor wears a white robe. The choir has white stoles. A white banner is hanging on the wall. And there are Easter lilies dancing all around the church. That tomb wasn't empty, it is filled with an Easter lily.

Pray with Children
Dear risen Jesus, help us to understand and rejoice in the presents you have given us. To you, we sing our hymns of praise, celebrate our hope, and dedicate our hearts. Amen

Related Music
"He Lives!" A. H. Ackley
"Christ the Lord Is Risen Today," Charles Wesley
"Thine Is the Glory," G. F. Handel

To Do Together
Paint, color, or draw a picture of the Easter story. Be sure to include Easter lilies in your picture. Read and look at Brian Wildsmith's book, *The Easter Story*, to see his Easter lilies in the tomb.

Easter 5

Symbol/Motif: mustard seed

Object: a variety of seeds and other small items

Sowing seeds is a common theme that runs throughout the Old and New Testament. The Bible teaches us there is a proper time to sow and to reap the harvest. A seed that is planted and nurtured will grow into something amazing. The mustard seed begins small, then grows and transforms into something big and beautiful. God's kingdom and our faith are compared to the mustard seed, which becomes large enough to move mountains.

Goal
Think that sometimes the smallest things become the biggest.

Bible Texts
Old Testament: Psalm 126:6, Ecclesiastes 3
New Testament: Mark 4:30-32, Luke 13:18-19, Matthew 17:20-21

Verse to Learn
For truly I tell you, if you have faith the size of a mustard seed, you will say to this mountain, "Move from here to there," and it will move; and nothing will be impossible for you. Matthew 17:20

A Children's Message

Come close. I have some things that are so small, you can hardly see them. Some of them are so tiny they might even blow away. Here is a lucky stone I found on a walk and a tiny shell from the ocean. Here is a bit of fluff from a flower and a little piece of gold. Here is a sunflower seed, a seed from a maple tree, and an acorn from an oak tree.

Some of these things are tiny now, but will grow and grow and grow. This seed, if planted in the right soil, given enough space, and given enough sun and water, will grow into a huge sunflower that will follow the sun. Inside this acorn is the seed of a mighty oak tree that can grow to be almost a hundred feet tall and can live over a hundred years. Or this acorn just might become food for a squirrel. That's okay, too. There is a reason and season for every little thing and every big thing. Planting an acorn is easy: first, find one that is complete with its helmet still on; choose a place with plenty of space where it will get lots of sun and enough water. Should you plant this acorn in the desert? No. It needs the nourishment of water. Dig a hole just an inch and a half into the earth, stick it in, cover it with soil, and pat it down. Then wait . . . and watch. To see this little thing grow, you will need lots of patience.

This acorn is like many seeds: if planted properly, taken good care of, and nourished along the way, it will grow into a beautiful plant that will provide food and shade and a habitat for many creatures. The acorn is like a tiny mustard seed, the tiniest of seeds, which will grow into something large and beautiful and useful. People are like seeds, too. Given all the right circumstances and care, the little seed that develops into a baby will become a beautiful person, a child of God, giving and sharing with those around her. That is why you are here today: to learn how to grow into a beautiful and loving child of God.

Jesus uses this tiny little mustard seed to tell a story about how faith as small as the mustard seed could move a mountain. If you have seen a real mountain, then you know how difficult that job would be. Jesus also compares this little mustard seed to the kingdom of God. It is small to begin with, but if it is planted and nourished, it will grow and spread. We can plant and nourish Jesus all around us to help his love to grow all over the world. That is how we will grow into beautiful children of God and increase the size of God's kingdom. Remember, the tiniest things can bring about the best, most important, and biggest changes in the world.

Pray with Children

Dear God, may our faith in you be like a little mustard seed. May we grow into young women and men whose "branches" contain the fruits of your love and kindness. Amen

Related Music

"All Things Bright and Beautiful," C. F. Alexander
"On This Day Earth Shall Ring," Gustav T. Holst
"Let All Things Now Living," Welsh folk melody

To Do Together

Plant seeds from a fruit, from a vegetable, from a tree, and from a seed packet. Label the seeds and then compare their growth. Talk about their need for good soil, water, and sunlight. Compare those needs with what people need in order to grow into loving children of God.

Easter 6

Symbol/Motif: shepherd

Object: a shepherd's staff or a toy lamb

Lambs are the young sheep in a shepherd's flock. They are gentle and especially dependent on the shepherd for water, protection, shelter, and places to graze. Shepherds were thus protectors, providers, guardians, and companions. The Bible also portrays them as figures of virtue and spiritual leadership, as poets, and even psalmists. Angels invite shepherds to see baby Jesus. The lamb was a sacrificial animal and symbolized Jesus and his sacrifice, his love for his people.

Goal
Recognize that the lamb is an important symbol of sacrifice and love in the Bible.

Bible Texts
Old Testament: Psalm 23, Isaiah 40:11, Isaiah 53:6-7
New Testament: John 10:1-16, John 1:29, Luke 10:3

Verse to Learn
The LORD is my shepherd, I shall not want. He makes me lie down in green pastures; he leads me beside still waters; he restores my soul. He leads me in right paths for his name's sake. Psalm 23:1-3

A Children's Message
The lamb is one of the most important animals in the Bible. We read about many animals in the Bible, including donkeys, wolves, cattle, dogs, fish, pigs, birds, and lions. But sheep are mentioned over four hundred times; and shepherds, who take care of the sheep, are mentioned over one hundred times. It's not surprising that sheep and shepherds play a key role in the message of God's word.

Sheep were very important to the life and times of people long ago. Sheep gave something to drink—milk; they gave something to eat—meat; they gave something to use for clothing—wool; and they could be traded for other things shepherds needed. Sheep need a lot of land for grazing. Sheep were not fenced in during Bible times, except at night, so caring for them was a critical job. Shepherds guarded and watched their sheep, fed and watered them, guided and protected them, all day, every day. Sheep are gentle and innocent, but also quite helpless and not always cooperative. They can wander off, get lost, and not be able to find their own food and water. Sometimes they can eat so much at one time that they would die unless the shepherd stopped them.

Some of the main characters in the Bible were shepherds, such as Moses and David in the Old Testament, as well as those New Testament shepherds who came to worship the baby Jesus in the manger. Jesus calls himself a shepherd, with us as his sheep. He takes care of us, finds us food and water, protects us from danger, and guides us when we don't know where we are going. We must learn to follow him and do what he commands. When we go astray, Jesus the Shepherd will search for us and bring us into his fold. All we sheep have to do is follow.

Jesus is the most wonderful shepherd, the Good Shepherd who was willing to lay down his life for his sheep. Today, Good Shepherd Sunday, we honor him. This Sunday comes soon after Good Friday, when Jesus was the Lamb who sacrificed his life on the cross, and after Easter, when he rose again for us and leads our way.

Pray with Children
Dear God, you are our Good Shepherd, caring for us and giving us what we need. You help us lie down in soft green fields. You lead us to quiet waters, not stormy seas. You prepare our table, filled with good things. We thank you. Amen

Related Music
"Savior, Like a Shepherd Lead Us," W. B. Bradbury
"He Shall Feed His Flock," G. F. Handel
"Come, All Ye Shepherds," Bohemian Christmas carol

To Do Together
Use the library, bookstore, or the Internet to find as much information as you can about sheep and shepherds, long ago and today. Where do sheep live? How are they cared for? How long do sheep live? What happens to their wool? Which country has the most sheep? Talk about the Good Shepherd, and draw a series of pictures of what it takes to be a shepherd.

Easter 7

Symbol/Motif: whale/fish

Object: a toy fish or picture of a whale

According to Genesis 1, fish, along with all the other creatures of the sea, were created on the fifth day of creation. Images of fish and the act of fishing are connected with the harvest of the people of God. While the sea suggests chaos and danger, the fish itself became Jonah's haven of safety where he could reflect on God. In the early church, the fish became a symbol—almost the logo—for God's church on earth and salvation through Christ.

Goal
Compare the story of Jonah in the fish to the Easter story of Jesus in the grave.

Bible Texts
Old Testament: Jonah 1:11—2:10, Genesis 1:20-23, Psalm 8:8
New Testament: Matthew 12:40, Matthew 13:47-50, Luke 5:6

Verse to Learn
But the Lord provided a large fish to swallow up Jonah; and Jonah was in the belly of the fish for three days and three nights. Jonah 1:17

A Children's Message

The Easter story has all of the elements of a great story: bad characters (Pilate and the people who betray Jesus); good characters (Jesus' mother Mary, Mary Magdalene, and the disciples); a scary three-day event (the cross and the tomb); and a victorious ending (the empty tomb). It is a story of power, greed, betrayal, and love. Many human stories ever since have mirrored that Easter story, but none has come close to its drama or its importance because only in the Easter story does Jesus conquer death.

God gives us exciting stories throughout the Old Testament that remind us of the story of Jesus. The story of Jonah has all of the elements of a good story, in fact it can be a scary story. There is a bad character, Jonah, who disobeys God, and a good animal, the whale, who saves Jonah. A man on the run flees in a boat; a storm at sea, and a man lost at sea; people destined to drown are saved. A huge city is saved from God's judgment. Wow, what a plot! The story has all the elements of a good adventure, plus greed, betrayal, arrogance, power, and, finally, repentance.

The Jonah story has some similarities to the Easter story. Jonah spent three days in the whale, and Jesus spent three days in the tomb. Jonah would have drowned if he had not been swallowed by the fish. God brings Jesus back from death on the cross, and uses the fish to save Jonah from death. But the main characters in the two stories themselves are very different. Jonah was sinful because he did not do what God told him to do. Jesus was the perfect, obedient servant: he did exactly what God told him to do. Jonah tried to run away, but Jesus stayed right there, faced his task, and accomplished his mission. Jonah could not save himself because he was human like we are. Jesus, because he is God's Son, rose from the dead. He lives so we can live.

Can you run away from God and what he wants you to do? No. Not even if you go to the bottom of the ocean, the other side of the world, or out into space. God knows everything, can see everything, and can do everything. God uses the story of Jonah to teach us to listen, to obey, and to trust that he will be with us throughout our lives. Trust and obey God just as Jesus did in the Easter story.

Pray with Children

Dear God, your power guides our lives. Your love saves us from our sins. You give us the hope of eternal life. We praise you with our thankful hearts and lives. Amen

Related Music

"Trust and Obey," D. B. Towner
"All Creatures of Our God and King," R. V. Williams
"Yield Not to Temptation," H. R. Palmer

To Do Together

Visit an aquarium, or use the Internet and books to get information on how many different species of whales there are. Draw different kinds of whales, fish, and other sea creatures while you talk about the story of Jonah.

Season
of Pentecost

Season of Pentecost

About the Time

Approximately 27 weeks; Pentecost begins 50 days after Easter and continues until Advent. Pentecost extends over three seasons of the year: spring, summer, and fall.

Seasonal Color

Red for Pentecost Day, gold for Trinity Sunday, and green for the season.

Pentecost Themes

Establishment and beginnings of Christ's church on earth
Outpouring of the coming of the Holy Spirit
Unity of the Triune God: Father, Son, and Holy Spirit
    God the Father, creator and source of life
    God the Son, savior and redeemer
    God the Holy Spirit, ever-present guide

Celebration of harvest; thanks and praise to God with instruments and voices
Preaching and spreading God's word

About the Season

Pentecost Day is among the most important festivals of the Christian church. Occurring 50 days after Easter, Pentecost is the birthday of the earthly church, celebrating the day the Holy Spirit appeared to the first believers. After receiving the Holy Spirit, those first believers had the enthusiasm, faith, and courage to spread the good news of the gospel throughout the known world. The events of that Pentecost are described in Acts 2.

The Greek word *Pentecost* means 50th day: Pentecost is referenced in the Old Testament, and there is celebrated 50 days after Passover. It is associated with Moses giving the Ten Commandments, which Jews view as the founding of the Jewish nation. Pentecost coincided with the Feast of Weeks, celebrating the harvest of grains.

In the New Testament, Pentecost takes on a new meaning. The crowd that has gathered for the Jewish celebration witnesses the Holy Spirit's coming to Jesus' disciples who are together in a room after his ascension. The wind, flames, and gift of communication make for a very dramatic entrance of the Spirit, promised to them by Jesus. The day of Pentecost is also known as Whitsunday (White Sunday), a day when many baptisms were performed and thousands of people came into the church.

The season of Pentecost focuses on the birth and growth of the church through the gifts of the Holy Spirit, identified in Galatians 5:22-25. Pentecost is by far the longest season of the church year, extending from 50 days after Easter until the beginning of Advent. It approximates the total time of all the other seasons combined, incorporating portions of spring, summer, and autumn. Thus, Pentecost is also associated with the planting, growing, and harvest times of the year. These themes are also reflected in Pentecost's color, green, which symbolizes the growth, fertility, life, and hope that Christians have in this world and in the earthly church.

Images associated with the coming of the Holy Spirit are wind and fire. The rush of wind symbolizes the power of God who breathed physical life into Adam of the Old Testament (Genesis 2:7), as well as the breath of spiritual life through the Holy Spirit in the New Testament. The tongues of fire are associated with the presence of God and purification through the Holy Spirit at Pentecost. The disciples also began speaking in "other tongues" (foreign languages) and performing miracles, which was prophesied in the Old Testament.

Key Bible Texts

Old Testament: Deuteronomy 16:9-10; Joel 2:18-19
New Testament: Acts 1:8; 2:1-13; Galatians 5:22-25

Pentecost for Children

Pentecost Day is a festival that marks the coming of the Holy Spirit, fulfilling Jesus' promise to the disciples. The day also celebrates the creation and beginning of his earthly church. Throughout the season of Pentecost believers explore what it means to be God's children, growing in faith as a community.

Pentecost 1/ Pentecost Day

Symbol/Motif: Alpha and Omega

Object: Any letters of the alphabet, for sure including A and Z

The Alpha and the Omega are the first and the last letters of the Greek alphabet. They refer to Jesus as the first and the last, the beginning and the end of all things. Occasionally, the middle letter of the Greek alphabet, *M,* is included in the reference, symbolizing that Christ is not only the beginning and the end, but that he also fills in the middle. And it refers to the Trinity as well: God the Father, Son, and Holy Spirit, being all things in the past, the present, and the future.

Goal
Become familiar with the first and last letters of the Greek alphabet, symbolizing the first and the last word of God, in Jesus.

Bible Texts
Old Testament: Isaiah 44:6
New Testament: Revelation 1:8; 22:13

Verse to Learn
I am the Alpha and the Omega, the first and the last, the beginning and the end.
Revelation 22:13

A Children's Message

The alphabet song starts with A, B, C, and ends with X, Y, and Z. The "A" tells where the beginning is; and the "Z" tells where the end is. Both are important, but the alphabet is more than the beginning and the end; it is everything in between, too. A and Z don't stand by themselves. They need every other letter because without the middle ones, we couldn't make words, sentences, or stories.

Everything has a beginning and an end. A book has a beginning sentence and a final chapter. The first sentence introduces us to what will happen; but without the middle, the last sentence will make no sense at all. The first day of school is in the fall and the last day is in the spring. These dates are important, perhaps the most exciting, but it's what we learn throughout the middle months that are really important. A first note and a last note don't make a song. The beginning and the end are important, but it's what's in between that helps us make sense of what happens at the end. The middle helps explain the whole.

Time has a beginning and an end. It is impossible for us to understand all of time because we were not there in the beginning and we are just a little part of the middle and the end has not arrived yet. We are just a little speck in that thing called time. God, on the other hand, has been around since the beginning, continues throughout the middle, and will be there at the end. God was, is, and will be forever. God is in the first verse of the Bible creating the heavens and the earth. God is in the middle, when he sent us Jesus. And God is in the last verse of the Bible, present at the end of our world. God goes even beyond the end of the world: the Bible says that God will abide forever. God is the beginner and the finisher, the first and the last, and everything in the middle, too.

Our alphabet has a beginning and an end, the A and the Z. The Greek alphabet looks very different from ours. The first letter is called the "alpha" and the last letter is called the "omega." Since early Christians believed God was the first and will be the last, they called God "the Alpha and the Omega." God is the A and the Z, the first and the last. But God is more than the first and the last—not only our beginning and end, but also everything in between.

Pray with Children

Dear God, you were at the beginning of time, and you will be at the end of time. You are the Alpha and Omega. Thank you for being at our birth, at our end, and giving us Jesus for the time in between. Amen

Related Music

"God Is Our Refuge and Our Strength," Samuel A. Ward
"O God, Our Help in Ages Past," William Croft

To Do Together

With the help of the encyclopedia, Internet, and other resources, find the first and last letters of as many alphabets as you can. Use the English "A" and "Z," the Greek Alpha and Omega, and many other languages to draw these letters as objects of art. Use any medium: pencils, markers, paints, or crayons. Choose a title for your works of art that will remind you of God, the creator and finisher, and Jesus as everything in between.

Pentecost 2

Symbol/Motif: anchor

Object: an anchor or a picture of one

An anchor is part of the equipment one needs to operate a boat safely. An anchor is something heavy enough to keep the boat in one position, regardless of the winds and waves. It is a necessary piece of equipment: without it the boat could wash up on a rock or drift out to sea. Anchors need to be heavy and durable enough to withstand any weather conditions.

Goal
Recognize that God is our anchor and foundation.

Bible Texts
Old Testament: Psalm 91:14-16
New Testament: Hebrews 6:19, Acts 27:29

Verse to Learn
We have this hope, a sure and steadfast anchor of the soul. Hebrews 6:19

A Children's Message
Since a boat floats with the wind and the waves, to keep your boat in one place you need an anchor. The bigger your boat, the bigger your anchor has to be.

If you are fishing in a little rowboat, you need only one small anchor; you might even get away with just tying your little boat to a tree on the shore. But if you are in charge of a great big cruise ship, you will need a gigantic anchor, in fact, you'll need three, four, or five of them. The heavier the boat, the heavier the anchor—they need to be in correct proportion. Most anchors are made of heavy, durable metals such as brass, iron, or stainless steel. Sometimes a big cement block does the trick.

Effective anchors have points on the ends, like claws that dig into the ground below the water. The points have to go deeply enough so that the boat stays put. Anchoring a boat is very tricky business; you have to know what you're doing because, with the tides and winds, your boat might smash on the shore or crash into another boat or drift out to sea. Anchoring is a lot more complicated than just parking a car on land. You need to take into account what is at the bottom of the water (sand, weeds, or rocks), the strength of the winds, the weight of your anchor, the boat's distance from shore and from any other boats. Some of those things you can see with your eyes, but some of them are hidden from view

Can you imagine your life as a boat? A beautiful, well-made craft floating in the waters of life? Do you recognize the dangers and the blessings in the waters around you? Do you have the skills to manage and sail your ship well, avoiding disasters and doing the job skillfully? You will need an anchor. Who would you want it to be? God is our anchor. God made your boat beautiful, and supplied it with all the right equipment. God has a plan and knows where we are going. We need to listen carefully to God's word, which is the map that will give us the right direction. God is our strong, perfect anchor, keeping us safe as we sail along through our lives, following, and obeying.

Pray with Children
Dear God, be our anchor when we are on the stormy seas. Be our guide when the way becomes difficult. Be our light when the path is dark and unclear. Help us listen to you, follow you, and obey you. Amen

Related Music
"When Peace Like a River," Philip Bliss
"Great Is Thy Faithfulness," William Runyan

To Do Together
Look in encyclopedias, on the Internet, or go to a boat store or maritime museum to learn about different boats and the anchors that are needed with each of them. Draw pictures of boats with their anchors.

Pentecost 3

Symbol/Motif: Bible

Object: several different Bibles, including a CD-ROM

The word *Bible*, based on the Latin word *biblia*, means "little books." Our Bible actually is a collection of 66 small books, with many authors, that was written over many centuries and reflects different styles and genres. The words of the Bible are from God who is communicating with us, giving us instructions and guidelines for living. The Bible speaks of God's word as revelation to humans, as sacred writings, and as prophecy from God. Some of the images used for the Bible are "lamp to illuminate," "a sword," "a mirror," and something that "abides forever."

Goal
Grasp that all of the Bibles used throughout the centuries are the Holy Bible, the word of God.

Bible Texts
Old Testament: Exodus 17:14, Proverbs 3:5-6
New Testament: Revelation 1:1-3, Hebrews 4:12

Verse to Learn
Trust in the LORD with all your heart, and do not rely on your own insight.
In all your ways acknowledge him, and he will make straight your paths.
Proverbs 3:5-6

A Children's Message

These are all Bibles, but they all look different. One is old, one is in another language, one is still in a box; and one you don't read but listen to. They are different colors—red, white, and black—and one has pictures. One of them fits into your computer. These Bibles all look different from each other, but they're the same: they are God's word.

All of the information in this huge Bible is on this CD-ROM. One Bible was read by someone who lived long ago, and another is brand new. One Bible is in a different language and was read by someone far away, and another has lots of pictures for little children to look at with a parent. Thousands of years ago, God told Moses to start writing the Bible. God said, "Write this in a book as a memorial. Write these on a tablet in your heart." At the end of the Bible, Jesus says, "Blessed is he who reads and heeds the things which are written." Throughout the Bible, we are instructed to read God's word and remember his commandments.

The Bible is not like other books we read. First of all, it is huge. Actually, it isn't just one book with one author; the Bible has almost seventy books and many, many writers. It's almost a library in itself! These writers didn't organize a conference and meet to decide who was going to write what and what topics should be covered. These books were written in pieces over a thousand years. We could call this book an epic. It has stories and poetry, it gives a history of God's people, and it gives advice on how to live. It's a travel book, and it predicts the future. It's even an architectural book, giving instructions on how to build things. There's a lot of information in this book, and it would take a long time to read it.

Our world is very different from the world that existed when these books were written. But that doesn't mean it isn't useful for us. God's word was good for Moses, and it's good for us. The Bible teaches us how to be good people and good Christians. That's what makes it holy. Its message is for people all over the world. It will still be used by people around the world hundreds of years from now! It's very important for you to learn how to read; then you will be able to read the Bible. You can use any of these—this old Bible, this one in a different language, and the one you can read on your computer. The message of this book never changes, because the message inside always stays the same. It tells us what happened in the past, gives us guidance for today, and gives us an idea of what will happen in the future. Remember that this is God's book—but

God gave us more than this book: he gave us the Jesus of Christmas and the Jesus of Easter. God gave us Jesus.

Pray with Children
Dear God, be with us as we read the Bible. Help us to grow in faith as we learn about your care for your people, long ago, today, and forever. Amen

Related Music
"Wonderful Words of Life," Philip Bliss
"Jesus Loves Me," William Bradbury

To Do Together
Choose one passage from the Bible and read it from different translations. If you know sign language, show how the verse would be signed. Have students "draw" the verse or write it in their own words. For younger children, ask them to tell what the words mean to them.

Pentecost 4

Symbol: boat

Object: a model ship, a small toy boat, or a picture of a boat

Although a boat can provide opportunities for pleasure and recreation, boats are often places of refuge and shelter from storms. A large boat saved Noah from the flood and a tiny one saved baby Moses from drowning in the Nile River. Jesus kept his disciples safe in their boat on the Sea of Galilee and a boat kept Paul safe on a voyage to Rome. The boat represents the safety of God's people at some very dangerous times. A boat, like God's church or kingdom, is a haven for God's people.

Goal
See that the church is like a ship with Jesus as its captain.

Bible Texts
Old Testament: Genesis 7:12-22, Isaiah 43:15-16
New Testament: Mark 3:9, Luke 8:22-26, John 21:4-8, Acts 27:9-44

Verse to Learn
I am the Lord, your Holy One, the Creator of Israel, your King. Thus says the Lord, who makes a way in the sea, a path in the mighty waters. Isaiah 43:15-16

A Children's Message
Do you like boats? Do you know how many kinds of boats there are? Big ones and little ones, narrow ones and wide ones, boats made of aluminum, wood, and fiberglass. Boats with motors, with sails, with paddles, even some that you have to peddle. You can ride in a boat or rest in it; you can dive or jump from one, and you can fish from it, too. Boats can be especially designed for calm days, windy days, hot days, and icy days. Some boats have their own houses—called boathouses.

All of these different kinds of boats have one thing in common: they all float. Long ago, Noah built a boat that he called an ark. God helped him plan and build it. For forty days and forty nights the rains came down and the floods came up. Even though everything on earth was destroyed, including all the people, Noah, his family, and those pairs of animals survived in his boat. Noah's ark is often compared to a church because a boat is a safe haven throughout dangerous times. God is the captain of our boat and the head of the church.

Early Christians thought the church was so much like a boat that they used the same word for ship as they did for their church, *navis*, and they built their churches in the shape of ships. The main part of this church building is called the nave, and it is like the inside of a ship. The church steeple outside is like the mast of a big ship. A church is a place where Christians sail the rough seas of life and survive the roughest of times. The captain rescues them from danger, keeps them safe from storms, and helps them find a secure spot to drop anchor.

Sailing a boat requires a well-trained crew as well as a captain, people who know what they're doing. Believers like us are God's crew. To be a working part of that crew, find out what your job is, learn how to do it, and do it well. Choose your boat and your crew carefully—and trust God, your captain, to see you through with flying colors.

Pray with Children

Dear God, you are not only the maker of our boat, but also its rudder, mast, and sails. You are our captain. You control the waters that surround our ship. We give you thanks for your Son, our guidance, and our protection. Amen

Related Music

"Eternal Father, Strong to Save," John Dykes
"Lead On, O King Eternal," H. T. Smart
"You Satisfy the Hungry Heart," R. E. Kreutz

To Do Together

Have you ever been on a scary boat trip? Do you always wear a lifejacket when you are "out at sea"? Read Acts 27 and imagine yourself in the middle of that storm! Then act out (or draw a picture of) the story. Include sound effects and plenty of wavy actions, as well as a prayer to pray before and after you reach dry land.

Pentecost 5

Symbol/Motif: Chi Rho (XP)

Object: a monogrammed object

The Chi Rho, one of the most ancient symbols for Jesus Christ, uses the first two letters of the Greek word for Christ, XPISTOS. The X is the CH and the P is the R. The *"XP"* refers to Christ, and it was used by the early Christians as a secret sign of their faith in Christ. The two letters, placed together in many different forms, have become a monogram for Jesus Christ. The Chi Rho can be used in any liturgical season of the year. Used in Pentecost, it refers to the expression and identification of God with his people here on earth.

Goal
Learn about the history and significance of the Chi Rho in the Christian tradition.

Bible Texts
Old Testament: Psalm 145
New Testament: John 5:24

Verse to Learn
O God, our help in ages past, our hope for years to come; Our shelter from the stormy blast, and our eternal home. (from hymn "O God, Our Help in Ages Past)

A Children's Message

If you have something monogrammed, it means you have your initials sewn or printed on it. A monogram can be put on many different items—everything from a beach towel to a pencil. It identifies the person to whom the item belongs. Some people monogram everything they own: pens, clothing, and tools. If you label your tools, no one will ever mistake them for theirs because the tools are labeled with your name. If your lunchbox looks just like ten other ones, it's helpful to have your name on it so that you can tell which one is yours. Some couples have their names and wedding date monogrammed inside their wedding rings. That makes the rings totally unique.

When you travel, you can buy a monogrammed T-shirt that tells everyone where you visited. You can buy a sweatshirt that tells everyone which sports team is your favorite. You'll see kids wearing shoes with characters on them, and lots of people wearing brand name jeans. You can buy just about anything with a monogram on it today: a tote bag, a coffee mug, pajamas, a jacket, or a book bag. They all have another person's face or name or letters on it. They show who someone else is; they don't explain who you are. That is more difficult.

Thousands of years ago, the Greeks used monograms. The Greek word for Christ is *Christos* (*Χριστοσ*). The Greek letter *X* is equivalent to Ch, and the *P* is equivalent to an English R. Together they stand for Jesus Christ, and when they appeared anywhere or on anything, it indicated those who had faith in Jesus Christ. "XP" can be found in Greek paintings and literature all the way back to the year 312. There are early pictures of Greeks going into battle carrying a banner or flag with the "XP" on them, meaning that they wanted Jesus to be on their side.

Around the world and through the years, that Jesus monogram has been called the Chi Rho. It doesn't matter what language people speak; that monogram abbreviation tells everyone who Jesus is. All over the world the Chi Rho tells everyone that Christ came into this world on Christmas, died and rose on Easter, and gives us everlasting life. If we wear something with the XP on it, we are telling the world that we love Jesus. Now that's a monogram like none other!

Pray with Children

Dear God, you have been with us in the past, and you are our hope for the future. Take care of us through life on earth and bring us to your eternal home. Amen

Related Music

"O God, Our Help in Ages Past," William Croft
"I Love to Tell the Story," William Fischer

To Do Together

Create your own Chi Rho design. It can be placed inside a circle, a triangle, or any other shape. Then design a monogram using your own initials in English or another language (particularly Greek). Decide which letters of your name to use, and then the font, size, colors, and what shape you will put it in. Where will you display either or both of your designs?

Pentecost 6

Symbol/Motif: circles

Object: three circles that are interlocking

The circle is an unbroken, continuous, connected line with no beginning or end. The circle symbolizes eternity, which has no starting point and continues forever. It also represents the earth, a globe, a part of the universe, or a sphere, such as a celestial sphere, or heaven. The circle of a ring symbolizes the unity of two people. And the figure of three circles together symbolizes the unity of the Holy Trinity.

Goal
Understand that three interlocking circles represent perfect unity, harmony, and eternity because they have no beginning or end.

Bible Texts
Old Testament: Genesis 41:42, Genesis 1, Job 26:10
New Testament: Luke 15:22, Colossians 3:14

Verse to Learn
Above all, clothe yourselves with love, which binds everything together in perfect harmony. Colossians 3:14

A Children's Message
I went to a wedding the other day; it was very exciting! Everything was perfect: the sun was out, the sky was blue, the groom was handsome, and the bride was beautiful, their friends and family surrounded them. Their marriage began when they said, "With this ring I thee wed. . . ."

This ring is like a circle. It is impossible to tell where this circle starts and where it ends because it flows into one piece with no beginning or end, just one continuous line. A wedding ring symbolizes the uniting of two people together, for as long as they live. They are now one. A circle symbolizes eternity because it seems to go on forever: it isn't a line that you can put a period at the end of. It just goes on and on or around and around.

A wedding ring has to last a long time, so it must be very strong. Gold is strong. Throughout history, gold has been used for special objects, such as crowns for kings and queens. People often use a gold ring in their marriage ceremony because gold is a very special metal for a very special day. A gold ring is like an offering of love to the other person, saying, "I will love you forever."

There is a kind of wedding ring that looks like three rings all connected: you put it on like one ring, but there are really three rings together. One of the rings is gold, one is silver, and one is copper. You can't possibly get them apart, because they were fused together. One of the rings represents the bride, another represents the groom, and the third represents their life together. Theirs is an unbreakable union. You can also think that one represents the bride, one represents the groom, and the third ring represents God, who unites them. The figure of three circles together, like this ring, also represents the three persons of the Trinity: the Father, the Son, and the Holy Spirit.

A circle is also called an orb, which can represent the earth. The cross represents Jesus and the circle represents the earth, and if we put them together it means that Jesus is the ultimate authority on earth, with the cross representing the love he gave to the world. God so loved the world that he gave his only Son to save the world. God's love forms a circle of Christ around us and around our world, and he holds us in his hands. What a beautiful marriage that makes!

Pray with Children
(Hold hands in a circle for this prayer.)
Dear God, please be an unbroken and unbreakable circle around our lives, so that we may live in perfect union and beautiful harmony with you and with others. Amen

Related Music
"Jesus Loves Me," William Bradbury
"O Perfect Love," Joseph Barnaby

To Do Together
Draw a shape that looks like a stained glass window in a cathedral. Fill in this window with circles of different sizes, colors, and textures. Entwine groups of three circles to signify the unity of the Father, Son, and Holy Spirit. Or draw three circles and fill them with things that come in threes, such as wheels on a tricycle.

Pentecost 7

Symbol/Motif: cymbals

Object: a set of cymbals

Cymbals are a percussion instrument, that are struck or clapped together. Cymbals are loud and are often used for marching and celebratory occasions. The Psalmist says to use the loud cymbals to praise God. But there is the caution in 1 Corinthians 13 that, without love, our voices are nothing more than clanging cymbals.

Goal
Explore the variety of ways people can express praise to God with musical instruments.

Bible Texts
Old Testament: 1 Chronicles 15:28, Psalm 150:5-6
New Testament: 1 Corinthians 13:1

Verse to Learn
Praise him with clanging cymbals; praise him with loud clashing cymbals!
Let everything that breathes praise the LORD. Praise the LORD!
Psalm 150:5-6

A Children's Message

Cymbals come in two pieces; you can't have one without the other if you want to hear what they're really supposed to sound like. A stick or a fork can hit one of them, but that is not the real cymbal sound. A strong person is required to play them because they are heavy. Most cymbals are made of brass, but they are not called a brass instrument, like a trumpet, because you don't blow wind into them; they are a percussion instrument because they are struck or hit together. Listen to the loud sound they make.

You won't hear cymbals played in quiet, heavenly, sweet-sounding music. They won't carry a tune or play a beautiful lullaby that might put a baby to sleep. No, they play music that is loud, exciting, and triumphant. Cymbals celebrate great events, almost saying, "Someone is coming! Something is happening!" Cymbals are played when there are lots of people around shouting and saying, "Wake up and listen!" Or, at the end of a basketball game, the band for the winning team will beat on drums and clash the cymbals together to celebrate. The cymbals say: "Hey, we won! We're number one!" You can be sure that you'll find cymbals in every marching band in the country.

The two cymbals together make up a very old instrument that was used thousands of years ago. David mentions cymbals in the book of Psalms: he recommends using them to announce and celebrate events and to praise God. He even told the whole nation of Israel to praise the Lord with singing, with the sound of horns, and with the clashing of cymbals.

We can praise God just by ourselves, too. We praise when we feel grateful and thankful, and we can make our bodies themselves into instruments, different instruments for different occasions and feelings. We can be loud like the trumpet and cymbals or quiet like the lute or the harp. Each one is important. Sometimes we announce and sometimes we reflect. Sometimes praise is so overwhelming that it bursts forth from our hearts and mouths like the cymbals crashing together, "Thank you, God, for this beautiful day!" "Thank you, God, for your wonderful creation!" Sometimes our praise is quiet and beautiful like a violin solo. Our purpose and responsibility is to give glory and praise to God using our bodies, the best and most beautiful instruments that they can be. In fact, we will praise God with our minds, our hearts, our voices, and our lives. So tune your instrument to be a perfect instrument of praise.

Pray with Children

Dear God, help us be the best instruments we can be for you. Perfectly tune us, teach us to play beautiful sounds that quietly or loudly, silently or together give thanks and praise to you. Amen

Related Music

"Now Let Every Tongue Adore Thee," J. S. Bach
"To God Be the Glory," William Doane
"Immortal, Invisible, God Only Wise," Welsh folk melody

To Do Together

Find a book that describes and pictures all the instruments of an orchestra. Talk about the unique sounds they make and how they are shaped. How are we all like different instruments in God's orchestra?

Pentecost 8

Symbol/Motif: door, doorway

Object: a doorknob or a handle

Doors and doorways bring us from one place to another. We must go through them to arrive in other places. A door opens and closes, is locked or unlocked, hides or reveals, keeps in or keeps out. A door is an entryway:

you cannot get inside without it. A door also keeps someone or something out; you can include or exclude. Jesus refers to himself as a door for the sheep or as an entryway to salvation: He opens the door for those who ask. An open door is an opportunity to spread God's word.

Goal
Discover that the path to Jesus and salvation begins with a knock on the door.

Bible Texts
Old Testament: Hosea 2:15, Psalm 24:7
New Testament: John 10:9, Luke 11:9-10, Luke 13:25, Revelation 3:20

Verse to Learn
Ask, and it will be given to you; search, and you will find; knock, and the door will be opened for you. For everyone who asks receives, and everyone who searches finds, and for everyone who knocks, the door will be opened. Matthew 7:7-8

A Children's Message
Knock, knock, knock. If we hear a knock on the door, we need to know where the door is. If we hear a knock on the door, we need to find out who's there. Can we open it? Do we want to open it? Do we want to invite that person in or do we want to keep her out? A knock on the door can stop you dead in your tracks.

Some doors are old, rundown, and unpainted, while other doors are neat, brightly painted, with a wreath or a heart or a beautiful brass knocker adorning them. In Italy there is a pair of doors 35 feet tall, made of bronze, sculpted with beautiful scenes from the Bible and so heavy you would need a crane to move them. A sculptor spent 21 years making those doors. But all doors, whatever they look like, keep people out and can hide things. People can do all kinds of things behind closed doors without anyone knowing what's going on.

Gates do some of the same things that doors do. Farmers have fences to keep their animals in. The fences have doors or gates to let the animals as well as a farmer's truck or tractor in and out. Big buildings and big houses might have fences all around them, with fancy doors or gates, through which only certain people can come. The President of the United States's house, the White House, is like that: people guarding the doors of the fence allow only certain people in. Entering some museums is difficult. One has to apply to get into a "scriptorium," a museum for old Bibles and ancient artifacts. Once pre-approved, a visitor still may have to register before being allowed through the locked gates and doors.

The Bible says there is a door to heaven, but we can't open it by ourselves because we don't have a key. Jesus said, "I am the door; whoever enters through me will be saved." How does that work? He will open the door for us if we just knock and ask to come in. We have been pre-approved! That door is an invitation from Jesus: When you receive an invitation to a party, you may be expected to respond with whether you are coming or not. This is called an RSVP. Christ sent his invitation to all of us on Easter. The door to salvation is open and we are invited to come in. It is a door of hope, of love, of peace, and of membership in the kingdom of heaven. RSVP and tell him you are coming.

Pray with Children

Dear God, thank you for welcoming us in as members of your kingdom. Thank you for opening the door to light and love, the door to the kingdom of heaven. Amen

Related Music

"Seek Ye First the Kingdom of God," Karen Lafferty
"Lead On, O King Eternal," Henry Smart

To Do Together

Read 1 Kings 7, an account of the architectural drawings of King Solomon's temple. Try to draw those doors along with some other doors. Then use your imagination to draw what you think is behind each of those doors.

Pentecost 9

Symbol/Motif: fish

Object: fish images: jewelry, a car fixture, a mobile, some pictures

Fish played a part in the lives of Jesus' disciples. They lived near the Sea of Galilee and some of them earned their living as fishermen. Jesus commanded them to become "fishers for people," that is, to go out and preach the word and gather in people to believe in the kingdom of God. Later, fish became a symbol for the early believers because the Greek letters in the word "fish" (*ichthus)* are an acronym for "Jesus Christ, Son of God, Savior. "

Goal
Learn about the history and significance of the fish as a Christian symbol.

Bible Texts
Old Testament: Genesis 1:20, 28, Jonah 1:17, Isaiah 19:8
New Testament: Matthew 4:18-22, Matthew 13:47

Verse to Learn
And he said to them, "Follow me, and I will make you fish for people." Matthew 4:19

A Children's Message
A little sign in your window or a small gesture with your hand can give people around you an idea of who you are, what you do, and what you believe in. Homes with a picture of a hand in

the window tell kids walking by that if they need help, the people inside will give it. A handshake can reinforce a special, even secret, connection between two people.

The symbol of the fish can be seen in many places today. People wearing jewelry or t-shirts with the shape of a fish, or putting a fish symbol on their car express their faith and let others know they are Christians. Where else have you seen fish? We are lucky because we don't have to hide our Christian faith. We can show it off and celebrate it! But at some times in history it has been dangerous to be a Christian. During the early dangerous times, Christians would draw or give the *secret* signal of a fish to identify themselves as Christians to one another.

How did the fish get connected with Christians? Jesus lived near the Sea of Galilee, where some of his disciples had been fishermen. The letters in the Greek word for "fish" (*ichthus*) are the first letters in the words, "Jesus Christ, God's Son, Savior," and the fish soon became a symbol for Jesus Christ. Many people of that time saw Jesus performing miracles and believed he was the Son of God. Today, if people wear or display a fish image on their car, they are proclaiming that they believe in Jesus Christ.

You can make a fish shape with your body. Cross your arms down in front of you, just above your wrists, and you will form the sign of a fish. In fact, you become part of that fish. Shake your hands with your neighbor and you become two fish together—a reminder that you are Christians who share the communion of Jesus.

Pray with Children

Dear God, help us trust that your Son, Jesus Christ, is our salvation. Thank you for promising to find and rescue us from the deepest ocean, the highest mountain, the most remote island, and the driest desert. Amen

Related Music

"I Will Make You Fishers of Men," Harry D. Clarke
"Let the Lower Lights Be Burning," Philip Bliss
"All Creatures of Our God and King," St. Francis of Assisi

To Do Together

Make a mobile, or draw or paint an ocean-scape filled with colorful fish. Cut a linoleum block or woodcut and make prints of fish. Go to an aquarium, the library, or the Internet to learn about the world of fish.

Pentecost 10

Symbol/Motif: flame

Object: five candles of different sizes

Fire is a part of creation, and sometimes is spoken of as one of the main forces of life. It is needed for warmth, cooking, light, and manufacturing. It is also an instrument of destruction and warfare, and can be dangerous. Fire is associated with biblical worship. It was used in burnt offerings to God, who frequently appeared in fire or a flame. God is understood to be the purifier of life and spirit.

Goal

Explore the importance of light, heat, and fire and their connections with God.

Bible Texts

Old Testament: Exodus 3:2, Psalm 29:7
New Testament: Matthew 3:11, Acts 2:1-10

Verse to Learn

I baptize you with water for repentance, but one who is more powerful than I is coming after me; I am not worthy to carry his sandals. He will baptize you with the Holy Spirit and fire. Matthew 3:11

A Children's Message

(If the fire codes in your community permit it, plan to light five candles as you refer to them.)

Today is the Day of Pentecost, the first day of the season of Pentecost. On this day we celebrate the coming of the Holy Spirit on Pentecost. The church wears the color red because the Holy Spirit came with a flame of fire, as well as a wind. Each person was touched with a special tongue of fire, and filled with the warmth of the Holy Spirit.

We appreciate the power of fire, even a small one. In areas with cold winters, buildings have furnaces. Even when the furnace isn't on, its tiny pilot light flame stays lit and ready to light the furnace when it gets really cold outside. If that little flame goes out, the furnace won't come on, and if the weather is really cold, the building's pipes will freeze and burst, and the building will flood.

God appears often in the Bible in fire to show strength. God led Moses in the wilderness with a pillar of a cloud by day and a pillar of fire by night. In the New Testament, John the Baptist told his followers that he baptized with water but that Jesus would baptize with fire—the fire of the Holy Spirit. Once we are baptized, the Holy Spirit lights a flame in us, shining a light for our path and guiding us in the right direction. We might think of the Spirit lighting several important flames in us.

The flame of wisdom, to make us wise in the Spirit
The flame of counsel, to guide us in the right path
The flame of strength, to bring us through difficult situations
The flame of knowledge, to inspire us to praise God
The flame of delight, to make us happy in the Lord

We need to keep our flame always lit. Guard your flame. Never let it go out. Use it to light our dark world.

Pray with Children
Dear God and Holy Spirit, make us your bright lights, learning about you, singing your praises, and sharing your love. Amen

Related Music
"This Little Light of Mine," African American spiritual
"Spirit of God, Descend Upon My Heart," Frederick Atkinson
"Though I May Speak," English folk melody

To Do Together
Light several candles at a family meal or at bedtime. Pray for wisdom, counsel, strength, knowledge, and delight in the Lord, and sing a song of praise and thanks to God.

Pentecost 11

Symbol/motif: harp

Object: a harp or an autoharp

Throughout the Bible, the harp is a musical instrument used on celebratory occasions, at mournful events, or in worship services. The harp sometimes accompanies divine speech, and in the Psalms is an instrument of praise. The harp, along with the voice, beautifully express love and devotion to God.

Goal
Understand that throughout history people have used music to praise God.

Bible Texts
Old Testament: Isaiah 30:32, Psalm 71:22
New Testament: Revelation 5:8 Revelation 18:21-22

Verse to Learn
Praise him with trumpet sound; praise him with lute and harp!
Let everything that breathes praise the Lord! Psalm 150:3, 6

A Children's Message
In order to play an instrument like the harp well, one needs to learn about it and practice, practice, practice. Then, maybe, with luck, after many years, one can make an instrument sound really beautiful. That was true in Bible times, too. David, who wrote so many Psalms in the Bible, played this instrument, and he refers to it often. The people of Bible times may have used the harp for family celebrations, for love songs or sad songs, and most often as an instrument of praise and worship. The harp can be used as a solo instrument, all by itself, or it can accompany a beautiful voice or another instrument. It can be used in many different settings.

At an orchestra concert, the harp is a difficult instrument to miss because it is perhaps the largest and most beautiful instrument on the stage. It can be as large as a grand piano, except that the keyboard is on the floor with the strings reaching for the ceiling. A harp usually is covered with gold and sparkles just sitting there. But wait till you hear someone pluck the strings; it is like a sound coming from heaven.

Fortunately, God doesn't require us to be professional musicians before we can offer songs and other music in praise. God doesn't want us to be nervous about performing for him, worrying about making mistakes. We also don't need to have an instrument sparkling with gold or a fancy Stradivarius violin made in Italy to make music for God. We are thankful because God will accept whatever we have to offer. Bad singing voices, okay voices, beginning violin students, accomplished pianists, God doesn't care what we sound like.

Music is a beautiful way to praise God. The Psalms say that mountains, trees, grass, meadows will all come alive with song. A creation filled with music: all day, every day! It's a concert around the clock, around the world, and we can tap into it at any second to be part of the continual concert. The notes and sounds we make show the praise and love in our hearts. Trumpets announcing a message, with cymbals clashing, will say, "Listen!" While our hearts sound like harps: ethereal, heavenly, full of love and praise to God.

Pray with Children
Dear God, thank you for this beautiful creation. Help us to be worthy of it, contribute to it, and take care of it. In everything we do, in everything we say, in everything we sing, let us praise you. Amen

Related Music
"Now Let Every Tongue Adore Thee," J. S. Bach
"O For a Thousand Tongues to Sing," Carl Glaser

To Do Together
Each day this week read Psalms 146 through 150. Talk about all of the things, in Bible times and now, that praise God.

Pentecost 12

Symbol/Motif: harvest

Object: small, medium, and large baskets

Throughout the Bible, a good harvest of crops was an indication of God's blessings on people; a poor harvest represented God's anger toward them. Hebrew religious festivals coincided with three different harvest seasons: barley with Passover, wheat with Pentecost, and fruit with the Feast of the First Fruits. Jesus sees the harvest as a time of opportunity: when the people are in need of salvation, just as the fields are in need of harvesting.

Goal
Praise and thank God for the abundance and blessings of creation.

Bible Texts
Old Testament: Genesis 8:22, Genesis 30:14, Ecclesiastes 3:1-8
New Testament: Revelation 14:15, Matthew 9:37

Verse To Learn
O give thanks to the LORD, for he is good, for his steadfast love endures forever. O give thanks to the God of heaven, for his steadfast love endures forever. Psalm 136:1, 26

A Children's Message

Here are three different baskets. They are all empty. Thanksgiving is almost here, so let's figure out how we're going to fill these baskets. The first part of the word *Thanksgiving* is *thanks*. Let's fill the small basket with some small things we are thankful for, like a lucky stone, a little flower seed or an acorn, a maple seedling, a penny, a strawberry, or a matchbox car. We can easily find enough things to fill this tiny, little basket.

Let's think of some medium-sized things to put in this medium-sized basket. We could put in a tennis ball, an orange or an apple. We could also put in a bouquet of flowers, a book, and a phone. We can put a lot of things in this medium-sized basket. What about this great big basket? Some big things would immediately fill the whole basket! A computer, for example, would fill it completely. How about a basketball, a toy fire engine, or a turkey! We have so many things to be thankful for, we could fill these baskets in a couple of minutes. And some of the things we are thankful for are too big to fit into even this biggest basket. Your family wouldn't fit, your home wouldn't fit; neither would a hospital or our church. But we are thankful for all of those things, too. Some things we can't hold or touch, but they also should be in here: a song, a talent, love, the earth! There are way too many things for just these three baskets. We would need hundreds of baskets to hold everything we are thankful for. And then we still couldn't fit them all!

These baskets can remind us of the small things, the medium-sized things, and the big things we have been given by God. "Giving" is the other half of the word "thanks*giving*." Since all of those things are gifts from God, how do we thank God? We can sing a song or say a prayer. We can love all the people around us. We can share our things with other people. We can try to be the best people we can be. Our baskets are overflowing with presents from God. Now we need to fill them to the brim with our hearts, our minds, and our souls. Then today will be a real day of thanks and giving and our lives will be a time for giving thanks to God.

Pray with Children

Dear God, you made everything. Thank you for eyes to see it all, and lips to tell how great you are, and hearts to thank you. Amen

Related Music

"Praise God from Whom All Blessings Flow," Thomas Ken

"This Is My Father's World," Franklin Sheppard

"Let All Things Now Living," Welsh folk melody

To Do Together

Each day, fill a basket with wonderful things. Use baskets of many different sizes. Keep them visible throughout the week, changing their contents and giving thanks each day for the items in the baskets.

Pentecost 13

Symbol/Motif: keys

Object: a key ring holding a variety of keys

A key represents the power and authority to open something. It also represents an invitation to something. By using a key, a person assumes the authority to accept that invitation. Keys can lock us in or confine us in something, but also represent the freedom that comes from being able to open something. Keys help decode messages, knowledge, and ideas. The disciple Peter was given the keys to the kingdom of heaven. In the Bible, keys sometimes are given to find knowledge and love.

Goal

Hear that Jesus is the key to the kingdom, opening the doors of heaven for believers.

Bible Texts

Old Testament: Isaiah 22:22
New Testament: Matthew 16:19, Revelation 3:7, Luke 11:52

Verse to Learn

I will give you the keys of the kingdom of heaven, and whatever you find on earth will be found in heaven, and whatever you loose on earth will be loosed in heaven. Matthew 16:19

A Children's Message

Keys are important. What would we do without keys? Keys are useful. They help you open the door to the place you want to enter. You can't start a car without one, and you are in trouble if you lock your key inside the car. A key allows you to open a locked box to look inside. Keys are like opportunities: they help you start the car, and oh, the places you can go. They give you access to new places and new ideas. Do keys always work? It doesn't matter how new or old they are or what shape they are; they just need to fit into a lock. Even a plastic key can make a toy work. Still, a key is useless if it fits a car that is already in the junkyard. Or if new people move into an old house and change the locks, an old key won't work any more.

Keys are a necessity. It's important not to lose keys. Without a key to the car, we would be forced to stay home. Without a key to the house, we might need to break a window to get in. Without a key to a safe deposit box at the bank, we would need to cut it open to get at what's inside. Did you know that church organs can have a lock and key?

Who gets to own keys? Grown-ups have keys and sometimes kids do too. There are brass keys, house keys, car keys, remote keys, spare keys, and hidden keys. Have you ever seen all the keys a custodian has? He can get into any room he wants to. If you have keys, you have authority and responsibility: it means you own something, or you can use something. Keys give you power.

Without keys, there are doors you can't open. There is a door with seven different locks on it. It cannot be opened by just one person. Seven important people have to be there, each with a different key to that door. Without all seven of those people there with their keys, that door will not open. Behind that door are the crown jewels. That's an important door!

Imagine a door to heaven. Is it locked? Who has the key? Jesus said that he would give his disciples the keys to the kingdom. He did not mean ordinary keys. Jesus is, himself, the key. He gave his life for us, and by doing that, he unlocked the door to heaven. We don't need a key; we're not locked out. He'll open the door and welcome us whenever we're ready. It doesn't matter how old you are, what color you are, who you are, where you live. You just need to ask, and Jesus will always be there to let you in. We have the key to heaven: we have Jesus. Jesus is our key! Don't forget that key. Study it, love it, honor and praise it. It will bring you peace.

Pray with Children
Dear God, thank you for Jesus, the key to the door to your kingdom. May we give ourselves entirely to you. Amen

Related Music
"All Hail the Power of Jesus' Name," Oliver Holden
"O For a Thousand Tongues to Sing," Carl G. Glaser

To Do Together
See how many keys you can find. In what kind of locks do they work? Trace or draw these keys on paper and decorate them. Draw some of your own imaginary keys. Can you draw a key to the kingdom of heaven?

Pentecost 14

Symbol/Motif: lamp

Object: a headlamp and a Fourth of July sparkler

Lamps are used in religious settings in the Bible. Lamps are also used figuratively as representations of light, guidance, witness, blessings, and life. Jesus tells the disciples that he and they are the light of the world, and their light should shine. The lamp symbolizes the good works of the righteous and represents the illumination of the Holy Spirit. Unlit lamps represent darkness, life without God, or death.

Goal
Understand that Jesus is the light of the world.

Bible Texts
Old Testament: Psalm 119:105, Genesis 1:3, Exodus 25:31-40, Proverbs 20:20
New Testament: Matthew 5:15-16, John 8:12, Ephesians 5:13

Verse to Learn
I am the light of the world. Whoever follows me will never walk in darkness but will have the light of life. John 8:12

A Children's Message
Have you ever been outside at night when it's so dark you can't see anything? You can't see what is on your right or your left, what's ahead of you or what's behind. You can almost feel the total

darkness. At such a moment you might want someone's hand to hold, or even better, a light. Flashlights are nice, but you need to carry extra batteries. Lanterns are fine, too, but they require some kind of oil to burn in them.

Many animals don't care how dark it gets. They are nocturnal; they have eyes that work in the dark. We need light to see, and there is a new kind of headlamp that has a solar-powered battery. If it is exposed to sunshine during the day, it will stay lit at night.

Before God made the world, everything was in darkness. Total darkness. No light existed. But God decided that there should be more than just darkness, and said, "Let there be light." God separated the light from the dark. Light became the day with the sun, and dark became the night with the moon. What a great idea!

The world was perfect until Adam and Eve sinned, and then darkness came into their world. But God had another wonderful idea about light: God sent Jesus into the world to be its light. Jesus is our light! He shines a path for us, like the beacon in a lighthouse or lights along the airport runway. Jesus' light warms us when we are cold. He is our headlamp in the dark.

We and our world cannot exist without light. We are children of light. Jesus tells us to be the light of the world, like him. He said, "You are the light of the world. . . . Let your light shine before others, so that they may see your good works and give glory to your father in heaven" (Matthew 5:14, 16).

Let's light this sparkler to celebrate being children of God. This sparkler's light is like our lives: it spreads its rays of light for a time but will burn out just as we will die some day. So while we are here, we must keep our lights burning and be the best and brightest we can be. With this sparkler, we can celebrate that Jesus is the light of the world and we are children of light.

Pray with Children

Dear God, light our lives so they shine and sparkle, creating a path to love, joy, and peace in our world. Thank you for your light, your example, and your love. Amen

Related Music

"This Little Light of Mine" African American spiritual

"The Lord Is My Light and My Salvation," Frances Allitsen

"Let the Lower Lights Be Burning," Philip Bliss

To Do Together

Each night this week light one sparkler, or one candle, and say a prayer for peace, joy, and love. Light a separate one each night for Jesus, like an Advent wreath's Christ candle.

Pentecost 15

Symbol/Motif: leaves

Object: a bag of leaves and other natural parts of trees

The leaves of trees are mentioned many times in the Bible in both a positive, beautiful way and a negative, punitive way. That dualism suggests health and decay, joy and destruction, and the richness and the inadequacy of the human condition. In the ancient world, leaves served as food, medicine, containers, baskets, and other useful things. In the Bible, leaves are compared to the lives and fruit of humans, as well as the blessings or judgments of God.

Goal

Explain how the leaf symbolizes seasonal changes and the seasons of our lives.

Bible Texts

Old Testament: Jeremiah 17:8, Psalm 1:3
New Testament: Revelation 22:2, Mark 11:13

Verse to Learn

They are like trees planted by streams of water, which yield their fruit in its season, and their leaves do not wither. In all that they do, they prosper. Psalm 1:3

A Children's Message

In autumn, as we rake yards, we find ourselves thinking about the fun we had in summer but also about doing things to prepare for winter. Lawn mowers may be replaced by snow shovels; swimsuits are put away and out come the jackets. We take screens down and put up storm windows. The animals also are getting ready for winter. Squirrels are madly racing around trying to find nuts to store for the winter. Some thicken up their coats and deepen their nests. Fruit like apples, pears, and peaches need to be picked and root vegetables dug up. The final crops are harvested as we prepare to live indoors rather than outdoors. People take the summer fruits and make jam from the berries or pickles from the cucumbers. Some people put extra food for the winter in fruit cellars. School kids settle in for the long haul of school. The leaves that we rake up remind us that summer is over, autumn is here, and winter is coming. They also remind us that life is moving on, from one year to another, from one age to another, from being young to getting old.

Many trees are mentioned in the Bible: oak, almond, balsam, olive, palm, cedar, walnut, sycamore, and boxwood. Some trees provided food, and some offered healing. Twigs were used to make baskets, and wood was used for building homes and temples. God used trees to teach us lessons. The first trees we read about in the Old Testament were in the Garden of Eden: the

Tree of Life and the Tree of the Knowledge of Good and Evil. Trees were involved in changing the world from good to evil. In the New Testament, the most important tree, a tree that also changed the world, was the tree that became a cross on which Jesus was crucified. That tree helped save us from death and give us everlasting life.

The falling leaves remind us that seasons change and that we need to prepare for the next one. Leaves also remind us that spring will come and buds will appear, blossoms will emerge, and leaves will break out in beauty. Trees remind us that God has saved us from sin and has given us a beautiful world. God gives us life and takes care of us in death. We are like God's trees: God plants us, helps us to grow and blossom, to be fruitful and productive, to be strong and beautiful in every season. God helps us change and adapt to every season of our lives.

Pray with Children

Dear God, thank you for the beauty of this earth and the beauty of the skies. Thank you for every detail of each season of the year and of our lives. Thank you for preparing the way for us. Amen

Related Music

"This Is My Father's World," Franklin L. Sheppard
"Joyful, Joyful, We Adore Thee," Ludwig van Beethoven

To Do Together

Search for many different kinds of leaves and other natural objects that fall from trees. Identify, describe, and display them on paper or in a box; or make a collage with them. Choose a favorite leaf. Frame it and draw, paint, or write about it. Find many references to leaves in the Bible.

Pentecost 16

Symbol/Motif: lion

Object: a toy lion or a similar animal

The lion was a greatly feared animal in an agricultural area where many people were shepherds guarding their flocks of sheep. The lion attacked animals and was unstoppable. The lion's roar was very loud. Even if people had not seen a lion, its roar spread fear throughout an entire area. Lions are sometimes called the "kings of the jungle," because they are so big and powerful.

Goal
Identify God's son, Jesus, as the one whose lion-like strength has overcome death and given us eternal life.

Bible Texts
Old Testament: Amos 3:8, Isaiah 11:6, Proverbs 28:1, Daniel 6:16-24
New Testament: Revelation 5:5, Revelation 19:16

Verse to Learn
The wicked flee when no one pursues, but the righteous are as bold as a lion. Proverbs 28:1

A Children's Message
If you could be any animal in the world, think about what animal would you be. You could be a lamb, with its beautiful white wool. You could be a white-tailed deer running in the woods.

You could be a blue whale in the waters of the Antarctic. Or maybe a hummingbird in South America.

There are so many animals—from tiny, quiet ones to huge, loud ones—that choosing one would be very difficult. Let's think for a moment about the lion, the king of beasts. If you were a lion, you would be very large and very powerful. You could hunt and capture anyone so everyone would be afraid of you. Because the lion is the king of the animal world, everyone would also be in awe of you.

Lions have been around for a long time. Thousands of years ago, the lion was associated with kings and royalty in the Bible. King Solomon wanted to have a lion on each side of his gold throne, along with six lions on the right side of the steps going up to the throne and six on the other side. Fourteen lions guarded that throne! They made Solomon feel safe and made him look like he was as powerful as the lion. People were afraid of him just as they were afraid of lions. Often a king would put a picture of a lion on his armor and weapons as he went into battle to feel as powerful and feared as the lion.

Remember the story of Daniel and the lions' den? Daniel would not worship Nebuchadnezzar, the king, so he punished Daniel and threw him into a den filled with lions. Everyone was sure he would die, but God tamed the lions and saved Daniel! The king was so impressed that he ordered all of his people to fear and worship Daniel's God.

Jesus Christ is like a lion: as bold and brave, as powerful and awe-inspiring as any lion, strong enough to open all the doors to rescue every person in his kingdom. Jesus is powerful; he is watchful; he never sleeps; and he protects us from every danger. Jesus is a king but is also a Savior. He is as strong as a lion but as tender as a lamb. He was gentle enough to forgive us and love us. Let's be the lion Jesus was: both powerful and strong, but gentle as a lamb. He loved us enough to be the Savior of the world!

Pray with Children

Dear God, help us to be as bold as lions in our love for you. May we be watchful, focused, and strong as we face doubts and temptations. Give us love and strengthen our spirits. Amen

Related Music

"Dare to Be a Daniel," Philip Bliss

"All Hail the Power of Jesus' Name," Oliver Holden

To Do Together

Watch the movies *The Lion King* and *The Lion, the Witch, and the Wardrobe*. Read any of the Chronicles of Narnia books by C. S. Lewis. How are the kingly lions in these stories like Jesus?

Pentecost 17

Symbol/Motif: moon

Object: A cloth or ceramic moon shape and/or a calendar with notations of the full moon.

In the creation story, God made the moonlight to rule the night. The moon reflects the beauty and providence of God's hand. The Hebrew lunar calendar was based on the movement and changes of the moon. "New moons" in the Bible usually meant that time had passed or a day was set aside for a festival to be celebrated. The moon gave regularity and rhythm to daily lives.

Goal

Learn how the moon helps us measure the days and the seasons, as well as our lives.

Bible Texts

Old Testament: Genesis 1:16, Psalm 8:3, Psalm 74:16, Psalm 81:3
New Testament: Matthew 24:29

Verse to Learn

Blow the trumpet at the new moon, at the full moon, on our festal day.
Psalm 81:3

A Children's Message

I'll bet your mom has a calendar right next to the phone. We need to be organized because lots of things that go on the calendar: birthday parties, dentist appointments, soccer games, piano lessons. A calendar organizes and reminds us of some little things and big things that are coming up, like Halloween or Christmas, graduations or play dates.

People didn't always have a calendar like we have. Ancient people had a lunar calendar; the word lunar comes from "moon." Their calendar year was determined by where the moon was in the sky, the shape it was, and how large or small it was. The moon was so reliable, so rhythmic, and so regular that people decided to use it to organize the year. There were 12 full moons a year. They could count on it. The moon was so important to them that whenever there was a full moon, they had a party! Every month they had a party!

We still base our calendar on the moon: if you look at your calendar at home, it will tell you every month when the moon is going to be full. The dates of many of our holidays are set based upon the new moon. The date of Easter is not based on when the schools want to have spring vacation. No, Easter is always the first Sunday following the first full moon after the first day of spring. The position and size of the moon is important in our calendars, too. Maybe we should have a party to celebrate every new moon!

The moon is a special creation of God. He gave the moon the responsibility to rule the night skies: to light a path at night. The sun and moon are the beautiful, bright, light handiworks of God's creation. The moon is so important and so reliable and so permanent that it has come to represent God's love and faithfulness to us.

We sing a song about the moon. It sounds like this:

I see the moon, and the moon sees me, down through leaves of the old oak tree.
Please let the light that shines on me, shine on the one I love.

God loves us and he shines his light and love on us. He provides us light for our feet to show us the way when it is dark in our lives or dark in our hearts. His light and love should fill our calendars and our lives. Look on your calendars to see when the next moon will be full. Be sure to thanks God for that moon, his light, his love, his whole creation. We would be lost without it.

Pray with Children
Dear God, thank you for being with us wherever we go. Keep us snug and safe within your strong, sheltering arms. Keep our hearts as full as the moon and the sea. Thank you, dear God, for all of your love. Amen

Related Music
"'Twas in the Moon of Wintertime," French carol
"All Creatures of Our God and King," St. Francis of Assisi
"From All That Dwell Below the Skies," *Geistliche Kirchengesang*

To Do Together
Find a family calendar at home. Does it show the full moon? Determine east and west directions from where you are, and where you can see the sun rise and set. Where and when can you see the moon rise from your home? When is the next full moon? When is the harvest moon? While watching the movements of the moon, talk about God's love for us forever.

Pentecost 18

Symbol/Motif: olive branch

Object: a dove with olive branch or an olive branch

Tree and branch images suggest nature, abundance, and God's providence. The Bible begins and ends with such images—of trees that offer fruit and life. God sent an olive branch to Noah after the flood, representing peace and love to the world. The tree branches at the very center of the Bible story make the cross of Jesus, and the cross ultimately comes to represent peace and life. Trees symbolize strength, power, glory, and honor; but they also represent God's judgment.

Goal
Know that the olive branch and dove represent God's peace and love.

Bible Texts
Old Testament: Genesis 8:10-11, Psalm 52:8, Hosea 14:8
New Testament: Matthew 3:16, Matthew 5:9, Revelation 22:2

Verse to Learn
Blessed are the peacemakers, for they will be called children of God.
Matthew 5:9

A Children's Message

When we look at the daily news, it seems as though a lot of people all over the world are fighting. Some fights are little and some are big. Some people fight with weapons and some fight with words. What can stop people from fighting and hurting one another?

God gives us so many gifts, but we don't take care of some of those gifts. We change them completely from what God intended—polluting water; wasting food; fighting when God gives us peace; getting angry when God wants us to love. But God is patient with us, hoping we will make good choices.

God has given us many chances for peace. Sometimes we accept the offer, and try hard, but still fail. Do you remember the story of Noah and the ark? God signaled a promise of peace with a dove and an olive branch. God also sends us a dove and an olive branch through Jesus and the Holy Spirit. Do we see it? Do we recognize it? Do we accept it? Most often we are too busy to even recognize that peace offering. Most of the time our world just keeps right on going in its own way, not paying any attention to God's promises.

We do use an evergreen tree to celebrate Jesus' birth and honor the tree (cross) that Jesus carried to Golgotha to save us. Think of Jesus as a tree of which we are the branches. Think of God as a tree with us as his fruit. We are called to work hard to understand how to live in God's peace, protecting, caring, and loving each other. That means being full-time peacemakers. Close your eyes and imagine planting a tree of love in a garden so that its roots will spread over the whole earth, its leaves will give shade to protect everyone from difficulties, and its fruit will nourish all of us. God will bless and help us be such peacemakers.

Pray with Children

Dear God, help each of us to be a peacemaker in this sometimes harsh world. Thank you for our world of beauty, love, and peace. Help us to recognize and care for it each day. Amen

Related Music

"Though I May Speak," English folk melody

"Spirit of God, Descend Upon My Heart," Frederick Atkinson

To Do Together

Plan, design, and draw a peace garden. What things are needed for a peace garden to grow and thrive? Read Matthew 5 and see what other blessings of peace Jesus describes in the Sermon on the Mount.

Pentecost 19

Symbol/Motif: potter's clay

Object: a lump of clay and some ceramic pots

Clay is a pliable, natural substance used by artists to mold useful vessels, pots, and other pieces of art. God is the master potter who formed and molded the earth during the creation. Humans were shaped and formed, molded and created in God's image from the beginning. God's people are like clay vessels that contain useful and precious jewels.

Goal

Compare a potter who creates art from clay with God who creates everything, including us, from nothing.

Bible Texts
Old Testament: Jeremiah 18:1-6, Isaiah 64:8
New Testament: Romans 9:19-33, John 9:6

Verse to Learn
Yet, O LORD, you are our Father; we are the clay, and you are our potter; we are all the work of your hand. Isaiah 64:8

A Children's Message
Here are some pieces of pottery. Do they look like pieces of art, or like things you would use? Do they look like they were made by an artist or by a beginner? It's hard to believe, but each one of these came from a lump of clay. Different people made them in different places at different times. One is from a professional potter, one is from a child, and one is from another century.

It's not easy to make a lump of clay into a beautiful piece of pottery. First, you need water to soften it up. Next, you need a potter's wheel in addition to your hands to soften and mold the clay into something beautiful and useful—if you are imaginative and skillful. After the clay dries, you can paint it with glazes to make it colorful. Then you need a kiln, which is like an oven, in order to bake it. You have to have the right kind of clay to endure the baking process; if it is not the right kind, it will explode in the kiln or will just fall apart. With the materials, the equipment, and some luck, you might end up with a beautiful piece of pottery, but maybe not on the first try. It takes a long time to learn how to make beautiful pots.

Can you imagine what it must have been like for God to create the universe from nothing? God molded this earth, the whole universe with his hands, shaping the water into oceans, the land into continents, giving the stars light and the sun heat. God had a grand plan, and accomplished it powerfully.

God also created humans, turning something from nothing into beautiful beings. The Bible says that Adam was a piece of clay made into a living, creative being, and given a brain and a heart by God. God continues to mold and make us, all of our lives. We can work with God to become useful and beautiful pieces of pottery, filled with honesty and love. Although we are molded by God, the potter, we are more than gorgeous pieces of ceramic art. We have something inside. We have brains, hearts, and minds that love God. God doesn't care which piece of clay we are made from or what shape we are; he simply wants us to be filled with love and as beautiful as we can be.

Pray with Children
Dear God, thank you for creating us in love, molding us to show your love, and equipping us to live that love for others, every moment of every day. Amen

Related Music
"Take My Life," John B. Dykes
"Spirit of God, Who Dwells Within My Heart," Frederick Atkinson
"Breathe on Me, Breath of God," Robert Jackson

To Do Together
Use a pottery wheel or your hands to form a pot or other vessel. Try to make it beautiful, but remember that God cares about us no matter what our vessels look like or what we look like. Our loving hearts and praise are the only things we can give to God.

Pentecost 20

Symbol/Motif: sand

Object: a sand dollar

Sand references in the Bible usually are made to indicate things that cannot be counted. Grains of sand are often used as parallel to the multitude of stars in the heavens and the seeds in the earth—an infinite number, too many to count. See Isaiah 10:22, Deuteronomy 33:19, and Romans 9:27.

Goal
Hear the legend of the sand dollar.

Bible Texts
Old Testament: Genesis 32:12
New Testament: Hebrews 11:12

Verse to Learn
Let the sea roar, and all that fills it; the world and those who live in it. Let the floods clap their hands; let the hills sing together for joy. Psalm 98:7-8

A Children's Message
If you can hold your breath under water, open your eyes, and dive to the bottom of the ocean—and if you are lucky—you will find many beautiful things there. One fascinating sea creature you might find is a sand dollar. An experienced diver puts on a mask, snorkel or oxygen tank, and

fins, and then swims around looking carefully at the sandy bottom for a disk and will dive to get it. Sand dollars are hard to find because they are the same color as the sand into which they dig and live. They are so well camouflaged that they're almost invisible.

Sand dollars are very fragile, especially once they have been dried in the sun. They are like an ancient hieroglyph telling us the story of Jesus. The sand dollar is a little sea creature that has amazing patterns on its flat shell, patterns that remind us of our faith. Look carefully; on the bottom can you see a bell and a poinsettia? The bell calls us to worship, and the poinsettia celebrates Jesus' birth on Christmas. If you hold the sand dollar up to the light, you can see through the shell in five different places. They can represent the five wounds on Jesus' body when he died on the cross. Some sand dollars have a sixth hole where Jesus' head would be, and so, look like a cross.

Sand dollars are flat except in the center on the top. Can you see an Easter lily in that raised space? It represents Jesus' resurrection. In the middle of that lily is a star that reminds us of the star the Wise Men followed to find the baby Jesus. If we break the shell open, guess what's inside. Five little doves. They are like the Holy Spirit coming down to show us the peace and love of Jesus.

A sand dollar celebrates Jesus. The star leads to Bethlehem, the flower celebrates his birth, the cross shows us his death, and the lily shows us his resurrection, the doves hover peacefully over us, and the disk's circle shape reminds us that Jesus' love is forever. What a beautiful treasure from the ocean!

Pray with Children

Dear God, you are as awesome as your creation! You are as infinite as the grains of sand on the seashore. You are magnificent in all you do. Spirit of the living God, inspire us to praise and love you. Amen

Related Music

"All Creatures of Our God and King," St. Francis of Assisi
"All Things Bright and Beautiful," English melody

To Do Together

Grab a handful of dry sand, and try to separate and count the tiny grains. Hunt for a sand dollar; keep it or break it apart to find the small doves inside. Collect other creation treasures. Lie in the sand and wave your arms to make sand angels. Visit: www.seashells.org.

Pentecost 21

Symbol/Motif: scroll

Object: a scroll and a Holy Bible

A scroll represents the physical form in which the words of the Bible were recorded, preserved, and passed on. Originally, a scroll was made from papyrus, parchment, or leather. The Jewish Bible is called the *Tanakh*, in which the first five books, the *Torah*, contained God's laws, including the Ten Commandments. Today, a scroll symbolizes the entire word of God: creation, the history of God's people, the laws, instructions, judgments, and love.

Goal

Discover that God's ageless word and laws were recorded on scrolls.

Bible Texts

Old Testament: Ezekiel 2:1–3:6
New Testament: Luke 4:16-21, Revelation 5:1-5

Verse to Learn

Take a scroll and write on it all the words that I have spoken to you against Israel and Judah and all the nations, from the day I spoke to you, from the days of Josiah until today. Jeremiah 36:2

A Children's Message

When we look at a scroll, we have lots of questions: What is this? How old is it? Where did it come from? Egypt? Is it an important document? Who would use a document like this? Someone important? What is the message inside? Why is it sealed? Who is allowed to open it?

Thousands of years ago, God instructed Moses to write down the Ten Commandments so that everyone would know what to do and what not to do. Since Moses didn't have pencils and paper, he carved the words in stone. Later, people began to write on dried out goat or sheepskins, called parchment. Small or big, after a letter or a book was written, it would be rolled up in a scroll. Each book of the Bible was written on parchment and rolled up in a scroll. These scrolls had printing only on one side of the scroll, so the writing was protected on the inside of the scroll. It took a very long time to write one. Very few people wrote them and only a few people could read them.

Our Bible is made up of 66 scrolls, written by different people at different times and in different places. We call each one of the scrolls a book and together these books are called the Bible. We believe that this collection of books is from God, which is why together they are called the Holy Bible. Our Bible does not look like a scroll anymore. Since the invention of paper, ink, and printing presses, the Bible comes as one volume with words on both sides of each page. There are millions of Bibles all over the world translated and read by people in over one hundred languages.

Some of those ancient scrolls still exist, protected and displayed in museums for us to see. Unlike them, our Bibles are new, available anywhere, printed in different colors and languages, easy to buy, and read by anyone who wishes. But the words inside are the same words as the words in those old scrolls. The words are God's words, telling us what's right and what's wrong. God gave us the scroll; Christ opened it when he died for us; and the Holy Spirit helps us read it. Our Bibles look very different from God's word given to Moses, but they carry the same message. Let's open it and see the message: love God with your heart, your mind, and your soul.

Pray with Children

Dear God, thank you for your words in whatever form they take. Thank you for your Son, Jesus Christ, who is your Word. May your Holy Spirit help us. Amen

Related Music

"How Great Thou Art," Stuart Hine
"Morning Has Broken," Gaelic melody
"O God, Our Help in Ages Past," William Croft

To Do Together

Make a scroll using special paper from an art or craft store and sticks or dowels to wind the paper. Or use any type of paper you have and cardboard tubes from rolls of paper towels. Write Bible verses or other words to share or remember on the scroll. Seal the scroll with fancy stickers or tie the scroll closed with ribbon. Consider making birthday or Christmas cards as scrolls with special messages.

Pentecost 22

Symbol/Motif: sun

Object: sunflower or any source of light

The sun is the source of life and the cycles of the earth's movement. The sun is one of the heavenly bodies, around which the earth moves. From earth we see the sun rise and set, indicating day and night. The sun represents the all-seeing eye of God and his source of light to the world. The sun may strike sinners, but is a blessing for the righteous.

Goal
Learn that God is the creator, source, and giver of all light to the world.

Bible Texts
Old Testament: Psalm 19:6, Psalm 84:11, Isaiah 49:10, Malachi 4:2
New Testament: Matthew 5:13-16, Revelation 7:16

Verse to Learn
But for you who revere my name the sun of righteousness shall rise, with healing in its wings. You shall go out leaping like calves from the stall. Malachi 4:2

A Children's Message
Have you ever seen an entire field filled with sunflowers? They not only grow to become very tall plants with huge "heads," but they turn with the movement of the sun. Their heads keep turning all day. In the morning they turn east looking for the sun to rise; at noon they face straight up because the sun is above them; and as the sun begins to set, they bend to the west. If you were a sunflower, your feet would be in the ground, your body would be the stalk and your head the flower, following the sun.

The sun rises in the east at dawn; the sun sets in the west at dusk. The words *dawn* and *dusk* are quiet words. Dawn is a quiet time before everyone is awake and before all the activities of the day have begun. And dusk is the quiet time when people settle down after all of the activities of the day are done. Both of these are beautiful, picture-perfect times when reds, yellows, oranges, and lavenders fill the skies. They are times when the sun rises and the moon sets (dawn) and a time when the moon rises and the sun sets (dusk). They are thoughtful times of the day, beginning and ending, almost mysterious times, too. We might wonder how it all happens, but most of the time we take sunrise and sunset for granted because we expect them to happen.

We can't live without the sun. It's not only beautiful, but also necessary for our lives. Without it we would freeze to death. Without the sun there would be no light; without the sun nothing would grow; without the sun these flowers would have nothing to follow. They would not even exist. We wouldn't be alive either because without the sun everything would be frozen. Like the sun, God is always there in the morning to greet us, and appears with the moon at night to guide us when it is dark. We don't even have to think about it because God is always there, illuminating us, comforting and teaching us, guiding and loving us. God is the giver of light, life, and love.

Pray with Children

Dear God, you are the true sun of the world, always rising and never going down. Shine in our hearts, warm our bodies, comfort our spirits, and guide us with your light to show us the way. Amen

Related Music

"Jesus Shall Reign Where'er the Sun," John Hatton
"God of the Glorious Sunshine," R. V. Williams
"This Is My Father's World," M. D. Babcock

To Do Together

In a place where you can see the sun set each day, position a board to stay in the same spot, perhaps on a fence. Each day mark with a permanent marker the exact spot where the sun sets. After a year you will see the change in the position of the earth and the sun. Find information in the library and on the Internet about the rotation of our solar system.

Pentecost 23

Symbol/Motif: Trinity

Object: a triangle (musical instrument)

Tri means three, as in the Trinity of God, the Father, Son, and Holy Spirit. In the Bible, three is a number of significance, reality, and completeness. Events in the Bible often occur in threes: Jonah's three days in the whale, Peter's three denials, Jesus' three days in the tomb, and many others.

Goal
Become familiar with the concept of the Triune God: God the Father, the Son, the Holy Spirit.

Bible Texts
Old Testament: Genesis 1:26, Jonah 1:17
New Testament: Luke 3:21-22, John 14:16, 1 Corinthians 13:13, Revelation 21:13

Verse to Learn
Do not let your hearts be troubled. Believe in God, believe also in me. John 14:1

A Children's Message
(Ring the triangle.) This musical instrument is called a triangle. You might hear it in an orchestra or a band. How many sides does a triangle have? This triangle has three equal sides. How many wheels does a tricycle have? Three notes sung or played together is a *triad*. Three voices or instruments making music together is called a *trio*. A skater who does a triple lutz turns in the

air three times. Three brand new babies are called *triplets.* Tricycle, triad, trio, triplets. *Tri* mean three. Three is the most frequently used number in the Bible. Jonah was inside the whale for three days; Peter denied Jesus three times; Jesus was in the tomb for three days. If something happens three times, it is not an accident. It is for real.

As Christians, we believe in another three: a trinity. A trinity, like a triangle, has three parts. In an equilateral triangle, all the sides and all the angles are equal. This equilateral triangle is like the Christian Trinity—the Father, the Son, and the Holy Spirit together make an equilateral Trinity. It's not like a tricycle, with God the Father as the big wheel in front, with the Son and Holy Spirit as the two in the back. That would also be a triangle, but a triangle with unequal sides—an isosceles triangle. No, the Christian Trinity is an equilateral triangle—all equal together, one complete unit. Three persons all in one person. Not triplets, but one person. There is nothing else like it that we know as humans!

One of the first things God said was, "Let *us* make humankind in *our* image, according to *our* likeness" (Genesis 1:26). The message was that God is more than God the Father. Jesus, God's Son, came on Christmas to make two, and the Holy Spirit came on Pentecost to make three. Luke tells us the Holy Spirit appeared when Jesus was baptized, when the heavens opened up and the Holy Spirit descended like a dove. Can you imagine it? It must have been beautiful and amazing. These three persons of the Trinity have different names (Father, Son, and Holy Spirit), and they have different descriptions, too: God the creator of the world, God the Savior of the world, and God the bringer of peace to the world.

The Trinity is with all of us every day. When you see a triangle, think of the Father, the Son, and the Holy Spirit.

Pray with Children

Dear God the Father, Son, and Holy Spirit, who creates, saves, and comforts us. Come to us on earth and stay with us. Help us to love you with our whole hearts. Amen

Related Music

"Spirit of God, Descend Upon My Heart," Frederick Atkinson
"Spirit of the Living God," Daniel Iverson

To Do Together

Think of as many words as you can that begin with "tri." Look up "tri" in the dictionary to check your list and see how many pages of words beginning with "tri" there are. Then do the same thing with words beginning with "uni" and "bi." How many things does each of them refer to?

Pentecost 24

Symbol: trumpet

Object: a trumpet, and, if possible, someone to play it

In biblical times, the trumpet was a loud instrument used to call people to worship and to war, to make proclamations, and to signal events. The trumpet also announced kingship. In Revelation, Jesus speaks like a trumpet to his people.

Goal

Appreciate the important role that music has played in Jewish and Christian worship.

Bible Texts
Old Testament: Isaiah 27:13, Numbers 10:10, 2 Samuel 15:10
New Testament: Matthew 24:31, Revelation 4:1

Verse to Learn
Praise him with trumpet sound; praise him with lute and harp!
Let everything that breathes praise the LORD! Psalm 150:3, 6

A Children's Message
If you hear a trumpet fanfare, who would you expect to appear? A king or queen. One trumpet solemnly playing a few notes can mean that a soldier, an astronaut, or a president has died. A trumpet might announce a bride before she walks down the aisle. Often when the trumpet plays, it announces, "Hey, stop everything and take note of what has happened!"

A trumpet sends out a message of royalty or victory, excitement or warning, sadness or happiness, the beginning of something or the end of something. A composer who lived in Italy a long time ago, named Verdi, loved trumpets. Many of his compositions included music written with the trumpet playing an important part. During one piece, Verdi wanted to have trumpets announce that the end of the world had come. So he wrote special instructions in the music to the trumpet players: he told them to quietly leave their seats in the orchestra and go to all different parts of the auditorium. When the conductor raised his hands for the trumpets to begin playing, most people in the audience didn't know that the trumpet players were all over the auditorium. When they started to make their announcement, it was so loud and the instruments were so close to them that the entire audience sat up straight in their seats and begin looking around. They knew that something important was happening in the music. Verdi wanted to wake everyone up and he figured out how to do that: use the trumpets!

The Bible, too, wants to announce something important: what will happen at the end of the world. In Revelation, when the door of heaven opens for us, we will hear a voice that will sound like a trumpet pronouncing judgment on all of our deeds. The trumpet will sound the voice of redemption and salvation. We hear the voice of Jesus tell us not to be afraid because he has already saved us from all of the bad things we have done. The angels are singing, "Holy, Holy, Holy, Lord God Almighty." It will be a royal event, a triumphant event, and an exciting event to celebrate. A trumpet will announce that triumph. The sound of that trumpet gives us reason to stop, look, and listen. We can praise the Lord with the sound of the trumpet.

Pray with Children
Dear God, let us praise you with the sound of the trumpet. Let our voices be raised with harps and cymbals, organs and flutes, drums and violins. Let every sound praise you. Amen

Related Music
"Praise the Lord with the Sound of the Trumpet," Natalie Sleeth
"Praise to the Lord, the Almighty," *Lobe den Herren*
"O Worship the King," Michael Haydn

To Do Together
Draw a picture of what the door to heaven might look like with Jesus on the throne and the angles singing. Be sure to include lots of musical instruments!

Pentecost 25

Symbol/Motif: vine/vineyard/grapes

Object: vines and a large bunch of grapes

Grapes were a large part of the agriculture of biblical times. Grapes were grown in vineyards and were both eaten as they came off the vine and used for wine production. A productive year of grapes meant a year of abundance and prosperity, obedience of the people to God's commandments, and thus his blessings. The wine from the grapes often represents the blood of Christ that was shed for his people and celebrated in Holy Communion.

Goal
See the connection between the grapes on the vines and communion with God.

Bible Texts
Old Testament: Psalm 80:8-9, Judges 9:27
New Testament: John 15:1-11, Luke 22:20, Revelation 14:18

Verse to Learn
I am the vine, you are the branches. If you abide in me, and my words abide in you, ask for whatever you wish, and it will be done for you. John 15:5a, 7

A Children's Message

Grapes are grown in a vineyard. A vineyard is made up of row upon row of vines that hold big clusters of grapes when they get ripe. If you have ever seen a vineyard, you will know that it can be huge. It can look like the cornfields in Iowa or the apple orchards in Washington.

Grapes will grow if they have the right climate and good soil with lots of sun and plenty of rain. When grape vines grow they spread all over the place; for that reason, grape growers plant the vines in rows and then tie them to stakes to tame them and train them to grow straight. Vines need to be pruned, and they need to be pampered. With all of the proper ingredients, vines will produce grapes that will be harvested, pressed, and fermented to produce wine or dried into raisins.

Israel, where Jesus lived, has many vineyards. Grapes have always been an important part of Israel's agriculture and economy—like cheese is to Wisconsin. Vines and grapes are mentioned in the Bible many times. Sometimes the Bible compares a vineyard to the kingdom of God. God creates the vineyard. The vineyard is filled with rows and rows of the people whom God has planted. He tends to them and trains them, protects them, and gives them sunshine and water. He nourishes and pampers them. We are part of God's vineyard; we are part of God's kingdom. We are God's children. That means that God will protect us, nourish us, and help us to produce luscious fruit. Without God's pampering we cannot do it. God takes care of us just as the grape grower tends his vineyard.

On Christmas, God sent Jesus to his people. Jesus grew up in that vineyard, was fruitful there, and later saved that entire vineyard from destruction. He died for that vineyard. In the New Testament, Jesus says, "I am the vine; you are the branches." We are not only part of the vineyard, but we are connected to Jesus. He makes us extensions of himself; he shares his body with us, which we celebrate in communion as we drink the fruit of the vine, the wine. As we drink the wine in communion, we celebrate God's care and love, Jesus' death and sacrifice. It means that we are the grapes in the vineyard; we are the children in the kingdom of God.

Pray with Children

Dear God, we are the seeds you have planted. You give us sun to help us grow. You give us moisture to help us flourish. You are the true vine. Give us faith to believe, love to grow, and hope to live for you. Amen

Related Music

"Let Us Break Bread Together," African American spiritual

"You Satisfy the Hungry Heart," Robert Kreutz

"When I Survey the Wondrous Cross," Lowell Mason

To Do Together

Search fields for vines from which to make a wreath. Collect vines, intertwine them, and form them into a circle. Search for pinecones, dried flowers, or herbs from the garden and other dried fruits from the fields. Tie them into the vine. Tie a bow on the wreath and hang it inside or outside of your home.

Pentecost 26

Symbol/Motif: water and a jar or jug

Object: a water bottle, pitcher, or jug

Water covers almost two-thirds of the earth. Water is a universal need: it is essential to life on earth. The Bible begins with God separating the waters to create the land and the seas; a short time later, God floods the earth, destroying it and then offering peace to Noah. Water functions as both a blessing and a form of God's judgment. Water has a figurative use in the New Testament, as well, when Jesus says that whoever is thirsty should drink of him to receive everlasting life.

Goal
Trust that Jesus offers us a drink from the waters of eternal life

Bible Texts
Old Testament: Psalm 23:2, Genesis 1:2, Jeremiah 2:13, Isaiah 12:3, Psalm 105:41
New Testament: John 4:1-26

Verse to Learn
Everyone who drinks of this water will be thirsty again, but those who drink of the water that I will give them will never be thirsty. John 4:13-14

A Children's Message
"Water, water everywhere and not a drop to drink" certainly does not apply to us. We are surrounded by clear, clean water in our drinking fountains, kitchen sinks, even our outdoor hoses. We have lakes and rivers to swim and play in and oceans that are too big to imagine. Water is so available to us that we hardly think about it. But people in some parts of the world are not so lucky.

Have you ever seen the Big Dipper in the night sky? Imagine surrounding it someone pouring water for everyone in the world. Water is essential for our bodies to stay alive. It is not just something we want when we are thirsty. Like plants and animals, we will die without water. Since the beginning of time, people and other living things have needed to be near water. Towns grew up around the local well; the oasis was an island of life in the desert; and cities thrived near rivers and lakes; the land along seacoasts is likely to be settled.

Jesus knew how important water was, too; he referred to it often. He talked about the body's thirst and need of water, but he also talked about the thirst of the soul. He told the Samaritan woman that the water from his well would take care of her body but also her soul. Jesus used ordinary water to wash our feet and quench our thirst, and he used holy water to be baptized. He invites us to drink with him and assures us that, if we do, we will never be thirsty again.

When Jesus was on the cross, he asked for water. No one gave him any. Without our asking, he died and gave us life. Without our asking, he rose from the dead and gave us victory over death. Without our asking, Jesus baptizes us and gives us the water of eternal life. Without our asking, he washes us into his kingdom. We cannot live without water on earth, and we cannot live in heaven without his water, the water of eternal life.

Pray with Children
Dear God, you are the water of life. Give us courage to live in your hope and love. Amen

Related Music
"For the Beauty of the Earth," Conrad Kocher
"This Is My Father's World," M. D. Babcock

To Do Together
Look at a map or globe and see all the water around the world. Identify as many lakes, rivers, and oceans as you can. Use the Internet to find out whether there is water on other planets. Read the story of the woman at the well in John 4. Then act it out, sitting next to a real or pretend well. Have cups and a pitcher of water handy.

Pentecost 27

Symbol/Motif: water, river, fountain, or spring

Object: a water fountain

Rivers and streams are popular places in the human imagination. We want to live near them, play in them, and write about or draw them. Their source provides a mystery and wonder. Rivers are geographic boundaries, sources of water and of life, and of God's blessing. Rivers are the places where the people of God gather to worship, and God's love is compared to a glorious river, which flows forever.

Goal
Investigate ways we are blessed with the gift of water.

Bible Texts
Old Testament: Exodus 2:3, Psalm 29:3-4, Isaiah 44:4, Isaiah 55:1
New Testament: John 7:38, Revelation 22:1

Verse to Learn
The words of the mouth are deep waters; the fountain of wisdom is a gushing stream.
Proverbs 18:4

A Children's Message

Imagine: at the beginning of time, the world was complete darkness and complete water. Then God gave light, and created dry land instead of having water everywhere. So God gathered the water in one place and created land in another.

We have oceans like the Pacific, seas like the Mediterranean, lakes like Superior, and rivers like the Amazon. Some of them are so big they can be seen from space. The earth is filled with deep mountain lakes, rivers running to the sea, and springs seeping out of hills, according to God's beautiful plan. Think of the many Bible stories about water: Moses parting the Red Sea, Noah surviving the flood, Jonah living in a big fish, and Jesus walking on water. These stories are about powerful waters and the powerful God who created them.

In many quiet places, without obvious forces at work, a little spring gurgles its water from inside the earth to the surface. At the bottom of a hill, in the middle of woods, along a riverbank, there is a tiny little spring that delivers water. If everything around it is very quiet, you might be able to hear it gurgling. It has a quiet power: peaceful and muted, but also constant and strong. The water from the spring knows where to flow as it meanders along, ultimately providing water that cleans us, nourishes us, and gives us life. But earthly waters can overflow and be dangerous. They can also dry up, leaving cracked and empty ground.

Jesus uses another kind of water to describe his love for us. Coming in many forms, his love provides nourishment for us as water does for plants. His love is like fresh water that washes us clean and gives us new life. The springs of his love never cease to refresh us, and they flow forever. God is the source of that fountain of living water of love: never-ending and overflowing.

Pray with Children

Dear God, you are the fountain of every blessing. You refresh our spirits and nourish our souls. You offer us goodness and supply all our needs. You fill us with love and teach us to give you praise. Amen

Related Music

"Come, Thou Fount of Every Blessing," J. Wyeth

"When Peace Like a River," Philip Bliss

"From All That Dwell Below the Skies," *Geistliche Kirchengesang*

To Do Together

Alongside a river, lake, or pond, play the H₂O alphabet game. The first person starts with a word about water that begins with the letter "a"; the next person thinks of a water word that starts with "b" and so forth. Read *At Break of Day* by Nikki Grimes.

Pentecost 28

Symbol/Motif: wheat

Object: a bouquet of wheat

Wheat was an important source of food and a product for trade in the biblical world. An abundant wheat harvest represented an opportunity for a thanksgiving offering to God. Wheat symbolizes the food that supports life, and thus it symbolizes life itself. Wheat is used to make bread, a very important food in Jesus' day and today. Jesus called himself "the bread of life."

Goal

Know that God's blessings give us a bountiful harvest, including Jesus' gift of eternal life.

Bible Texts

Old Testament: Exodus 34:22, Isaiah 27:12
New Testament: Matthew 13:24-30, 37

Verse to Learn

Jesus said to them, "I am the bread of life. Whoever comes to me will never be hungry, and whoever believes in me will never be thirsty." John 6:35

A Children's Message

Bouquets are usually made of flowers. This is not a bouquet of fresh flowers or even dried flowers: it is a bouquet of wheat. It may not be as beautiful as flowers, but it has more value than mere beauty: it will nourish our bodies. The little seeds from plants like these will end up in your cereal or bread. Before this bouquet is ready to be picked, the farmer first clears the field, plants the seeds, waters it, hopes for sunshine, weeds between the rows, and watches it grow. Around this time of year he harvests the plants and takes all of the little seeds out. He sells those seeds and eventually it ends up being eaten. From seed to sandwich is a long, hard, and risky process; without the farmer's work and good weather the wheat crop will not grow and prosper.

Jesus says that the field of wheat is like the world, and each of us is like a wheat plant—like the sons and daughters of God's kingdom. Jesus, the farmer, has cleared, prepared, and planted the field. He plants us when he thinks the time is right. There are many dangers along the way, but he protects his plants. Maybe there doesn't seem to be enough water, but he says we will not thirst; maybe there's not enough sunshine, but he sends us light in the world. Jesus says angels will send water and sunshine to nourish us and help us grow into strong, healthy plants. Maybe nobody tills the ground and weeds choke us, but he says that he clears the path. Our field will sometimes be filled with weeds and wildflowers, but he will show us the way. He tells us to watch out because there are dangers along the way, but not to fear since he protects us.

At harvest time, God harvests the crops, gathering us up as his children, for we are all part of his family, his wheat harvest. God gives us the wheat for the true bread from heaven, and that is Jesus. He is bread for our lives. Jesus says, "I am the bread of life. Whoever comes to me will never be hungry, and whoever believes in me will never be thirsty" (John 6:35).

Pray with Children
Dear God, thank you for giving us that field of wheat and planting us seeds here. Nurture us with love to grow. Harvest us as your people to live with you in your kingdom. Amen

Related Music
"We Plow the Fields and Scatter," Johann Schulz
"You Satisfy the Hungry Heart," Robert E. Kreutz
"Let All Things Now Living," Welsh folk melody

To Do Together
Gather a large bouquet of wheat and tie it with a beautiful ribbon. Use it as a centerpiece for your dining room table for a few weeks. Do the same with weeds and wildflowers, but remember that no matter how pretty they are, they are not food and cannot sustain life. Thank God for plants of beauty and life-sustaining food.